THE POWER O

THE AUTHOR

Charles Perry McCormick was long recognized as a pioneer in human relations, a man with the insight to perceive that human dignity must be acknowledged and understood as an essential factor in achieving effective management-labor relations. His philosophy in this field was best expressed in his book, "The Power of People," first published in 1949.

Born in Morelia, Mexico, on June 9, 1896, C. P. McCormick received his preliminary education in Mexico, Puerto Rico, France, Massachusetts, Alabama and Virginia, accompanying his father, the Reverend Hugh Pendleton McCormick, on his various missionary assignments. In 1912, after the family had settled in Baltimore, young McCormick started summer work at McCormick and Company while attending high school. His active service with McCormick continued for 57 years until his retirement as Chairman of the Board in 1969. He served as Emeritus Chairman until his death on June 16, 1970.

Among the responsible civic and governmental positions Charles P. McCormick occupied during a life of service and dedication were:

Chairman, Board of Regents, University of Maryland
Chairman, Baltimore Civic Center Commission
U. S. Employer Delegate, International Labor Organization, Geneva, Switzerland, 1949-1955
Chairman, Federal Reserve Bank of Richmond
Chairman, National Heart Fund, 1958 and 1959
Business Advisory Council, U. S. Department of Commerce
Board of Trustees, American University
National Director, Boys Club of America

Among the honors he received were:

Distinguished Service Award, National Conference of Christians and Jews, 1958
Big Brother of the Year, awarded jointly by Big Brothers of Baltimore, Inc., and Jewish Big Brother League
Man of the Year Award, Advertising Club of Baltimore, 1962
Golden Deeds Award, Exchange Club, 1958
Gantt Gold Medal, 1960 from the American Management Association and American Society of Mechanical Engineers, 1960

THE POWER
OF PEOPLE

Multiple Management
Up to Date

————————————

By CHARLES P. McCORMICK
Author of "Multiple Management"

Produced for McCormick by Penguin Books

CONTENTS

TODAY'S VIEW
by Harry K. Wells, President, McCormick & Company, Inc.

THE original publication of "The Power of People" in 1949 marked the seventeenth year of the development of Multiple Management in the United States. Since then, there have been ten printings, as well as a soft-cover edition issued in 1952. For those who have entered the business world following these early publications, "The Power of People" by Charles P. McCormick is being reissued in its original text.

Perhaps, the future will see a sequel version showing how Multiple Management has been adapted to and integrated into the complex, worldwide structure of our company in today's world.

For the time being, we can only stress that "The Power of People" is supremely valid and relevant today. Although current challenges may come from new areas, or areas which have acquired new emphasis, people retain the same basic aims, intensified by a larger awareness of worldwide social values, problems in economics, environment and other stresses. This awareness in itself has made the philosophy and practice of Multiple Management and its continuing principles a dynamic factor in our day-to-day evaluation and in our long-range planning.

Even though many of the specific growth problems of the period behind us are successfully resolved, new threats to the enjoyment of our progress arise daily. As the world business community expands and our organization becomes more intricate, so do the problems and the search for solutions.

To aid us, we now have sophisticated new tools at our disposal. Management planning has become a science. Electronic information systems provide precise and instant data. The communications network and jet travel have contributed, too, to our effectiveness as managers of industry. Each of these, however, merely serves to emphasize that our lasting success depends on the individual realizing his fullest capabilities, and the recognition of these capabilities by management.

One of the paramount benefits arising from Multiple Management, as created by Charles P. McCormick, is effective participation at all levels of employment, through a system of functioning boards. Because each board is both concerned and informed on the problems and potentials in its area of involvement, all members are fully prepared to contribute toward the betterment of their company, their fellow associates and their community. Too, every member learns much about the company and, in doing so, develops a potential for personal growth and management breadth.

Participation through Multiple Management is the keynote of our continuing philosophy. "The Power of People" gives us one of the tools most widely used in maintaining the stability and extending the stature of our company. It is a power that enables us to benefit from the past, relate to the present and plan for the future—together.

HARRY K. WELLS, 1973

PREFACE

IN THE seventeen years since Multiple Management was established at McCormick & Company, some of the best students of human relations throughout the world have come to see us to learn more about what we are doing here. The exchange of ideas has stimulated my thinking about people and has broadened my concept of our original plan.

That's why I call this book, "The Power of People." What I have to say here is more than a message to businessmen. It is a challenge to all Americans to recognize the impact of people on business, government, and our free American society. I offer here out of our experience what we hope will be constructive suggestions as to what can be done to meet this challenge.

In 1937, Harper & Brothers published a book I wrote describing some of the pioneering in human relations we were doing at McCormick & Company under the title "Multiple Management."

When the publishers asked me last year to revise that book and bring it up to date because of continued and increased interest in the subject, I set to work to do so. But I soon found that I had more to say than a mere revised description of Multiple Management.

That is why I have attempted here to pass on to a new generation a lesson regarding the power of the people which I believe this story demonstrates.

CHARLES P. McCORMICK.

Baltimore, Md.
April 10, 1949.

FOREWORD

S INCE my father wrote "The Power of People," McCormick has grown at a very rapid rate and now includes nearly thirty divisions and subsidiaries throughout the world. The Multiple Management philosophy has been a major motivating force in the development of these profit centers and in the expansion of the company as a whole.

Hundreds of other companies, including those of major stature throughout the world, have been interested in how McCormick has coped with its extraordinary growth and maintained the principles of Multiple Management.

I feel that the Multiple Management philosophy is more meaningful today than ever before. Today's younger generation—whether consumers or management participants—are eager for the freedom of self-expression and participation. On the whole, they are bright, well educated and full of ideas.

For the aggressive company that really believes change is not only a way of life, but should be encouraged, the recognition of THE POWER OF PEOPLE can generate the climate of faith and opportunity which breeds employee satisfaction and company success.

C. P. McCormick, Jr., 1973

A WORKER SPEAKS

YES, I guess you could call me one of the old-timers here. I first came to work for McCormick & Company in 1904, when Mr. Willoughby McCormick, who started the business originally, was just getting up steam. I worked here about four years the first time and left to take a job in another company. Why? Well, the pay here was pretty low then and, to tell you the truth, the working conditions weren't too good either. I can give you one idea; the place wasn't as clean and orderly as it is now. You can see that the plant shines like a new pin now, but back in those times we were coated with pepper dust by night and there weren't any showers where we could clean up before leaving. Then, too, the wage scale was below most of the industries around here, and you didn't have much protection against being laid off either.

"Well, to make a long story short, after working for this other company for a while, I drifted back here. I liked the wages at the other place but I wanted to get married and there wasn't any place to live in this other town, so when I came back to Baltimore I headed back to the old job the way people will.

"Now I'll tell you something about the management here before Charlie McCormick took over as president in 1932. Mr. Willoughby McCormick had started this business himself. He worked very hard at it, and in his way of thinking this was his business and nobody else's. The workers were just like part of the machinery or the building, and they weren't paid to think. In fact, Mr. McCormick made that pretty clear to

*everyone including his foremen and superintendents. Now,
this does not mean that Willoughby McCormick was a bad
boss—I don't want you to get that idea at all. He was simply
like a lot of the company presidents of that particular period.
I hate to say this, but I guess many of them are still like that
even today. Willoughby was a good church member, gave
money to charity and all that, but he had no feeling at all for
human relations in his business as we know them here today.*

*"To give you some idea of the way workers felt then, let
me tell you about the old signal system. We all got to know
that Mr. Willoughby could be counted upon to come out of
his office two or three times a day and make a quick trip
through the plant and office. He liked to get the feeling that
everything was humming right along. Well, the workers
caught onto that pretty quick. They wanted to keep their jobs
and they learned that about all they had to do was to look
good for a few minutes every day when he toured the plant.
Well, sir, we had about the most elaborate signal system since
Indian smoke signals. Every time Mr. Willoughby left his
office there was a whole series of secret code signals worked
out by beating on the steam pipes and jangling the telephone,
which let every department know 'the old man' was on his
way through. Boy, we had to work so hard to make him think
we looked good when he made those visits through the plant
that we just had to let down the rest of the day.*

*"That's just one example of the way the workers acted then.
I got to feeling the management and workers were playing a
sort of a cat-and-mouse game. The workers thought that management was out to beat them down and get as much work out
of them as they could, at just as little pay. The management
thought that the workers were out to loaf around and take it
easy and had to be watched all the time. There was no trust,
and as a result you can imagine that production wasn't too*

hot. The only way we got things done was to stand over people as though they were prisoners or something and make sure that they didn't break any rules.

"And believe me we really had some rules—what you could do, but mostly what you couldn't do. There weren't any written employee personnel policies, and there weren't any real principles of co-operation laid down, mostly because management didn't want to commit itself. 'Don't make any promises,' Mr. Willoughby confidentially told me one day. 'Then you'll never have your neck stuck out on things.' Well, maybe that was all right for management, but it was a little tough on us.

"Mr. Willoughby had his share of bad luck. His plant burned down completely in the big Baltimore fire, but he had a lot of courage and determination and built it up again. He really had a lot of moral courage, that man. His motto was: 'Make the best—someone will buy it.' He did make extremely fine quality products and his business moved along pretty well as the country grew. But it never completely realized its potential. For the most part, as far as the workers were concerned, it was just another place to work. We drew our pay, such as it was, and that was about all we knew or cared about the company.

"Charlie McCormick came to work here about 1912 in the summers and in 1918 started full time. He was just a pleasant enough young fellow, we thought. We got to know him pretty well because he worked all through the plant. He and his uncle used to argue a lot, and I know that Mr. Willoughby used to tell him the same thing he told the rest of us: 'This is my business, and I'll do the thinking for it. You are not paid to think; you are paid to work.'

"I know Willoughby fired Charlie four or five times because Charlie used to speak up and try to get across some of his ideas—and took up for the workers when they were right.

"*Because nobody felt sure of anything, our employee turn-over was pretty high. You see, spice and extract and tea manu-facturing is a sort of a seasonal business. Under Mr. Wil-loughby, we hired and laid off about three times a year. You can imagine the net results of this program, plus the fact that Mr. Willoughby maintained a sort of 'Employee-Gestapo' through his pet supervisors. All of this combined made the workers sore as hell.*

"*Mr. Willoughby passed away in the deep depression days of 1932, and the Board of Directors elected Charlie McCor-mick as president of the company. The company was in pretty bad shape by that time. We'd been losing money for several years, production was down, costs were up, there were further rumors of wage cuts, and the morale of all the people who worked there was just about as low as it could be. So when Charlie McCormick took over, the place was really buzzing from top to bottom about what would happen. We soon found out!*

"*The first thing Charlie did was to call together all the em-ployees. He told us things we'd never known before about the company and told the department heads things about their departments that they'd never known before either. He got us interested and he started us thinking about our jobs. Then he said something I have never forgotten. He said he was going to replace fear with faith in this business. He believed in people and figured if they got a square deal they would work along with him to help build the business together as a team.*

"*Right there Charlie announced that he was going to in-crease wages 10 per cent and cut the time down from 56 to 45 hours a week. A little later he told us about his '40-40' idea— 40 hours a week and 40 cents per hour minimum. That was to be a kind of goal we would work toward together. Now re-*

member, this was before the laws on wages and hours and all that sort of thing.

"Well, sir, a lot of people around Baltimore then thought Charlie was just crazy. We all got a big kick out of it a couple of years ago when the Baltimore businessmen presented Charlie a big certificate in recognition of his pioneering in human relations. You see, other businesses both in this town and in other cities finally began to do some of the same things in human relations, but back in 1932 what happened at McCormick's was big news.

"Did Charlie's ideas work? I'll say they did. Despite skeptics both in and out of the plant, production stepped up, costs fell, and at the end of that first year McCormick & Company went out of the red and into the black. It's stayed in the black ever since.

"All this happened seventeen years ago. Today McCormick & Company is the largest spice and extract house in the world, with branches scattered all over the country. Two years ago we acquired the fine old house of A. Schilling and Company in San Francisco.

"But the biggest change came not in dollars and cents but in the way people are treated and how people feel about the company. The new spirit has come from this thing called 'Multiple Management' that Charlie started back there in 1932. Now we all feel we are working as a team instead of each man for himself only. A few years ago, when one of the fellows down in the carpenter shop won a President's award at one of our monthly employee meetings, Charlie asked him just for fun to give his definition of Multiple Management from the point of view of an average worker. He said: 'The way I feel about Multiple Management is that it's like being in business for yourself on somebody else's money.'

"*That pretty well summed up the attitudes of all of us. It's more than just good personnel policies. Sure, we have a lot of nice things in the way of wages and benefits. Our pay has climbed way up from the old days and matches anything we could get in the same kind of job anywhere around town. In addition to that we've got a pension plan for everybody that the company pays all the premiums on. We've got security because the firm gives forty-eight weeks of work a year to the top 90% of the organization, based on merit and length of service. And we've got profit-sharing so that when we all do a good job we share in the rewards of it. Our vacations are good and we have rest periods twice a day so with lunch nobody has to work more than two hours without a break from their machines.*

"*But most important of all, we're part of the whole show. Working here, you get the idea that people really want to listen to you and have you join in things instead of just being part of the machinery around the place. Many years ago we kicked out the time clocks because we just didn't need them any more. We discovered that working on trust, though still following through, of course, with good supervision, keeps production just as high. It's because we're pretty happy while at work that this place is different from somewhere else. Naturally, something may come up that we don't like, but we don't have to grit our teeth and bear it. Instead, we're encouraged to air the matter and work it out together.*

"*Under Multiple Management I've seen some of the fellows around here change a lot, especially one man—the plant superintendent who in Mr. Willoughby's time used to head the company 'Gestapo.' This guy kept notes in a little black book on everyone who worked here, and he would go over them with Mr. Willoughby every once in a while. Then a lot of folks would be hauled into the front office and bawled out good.*

"Well, you can imagine this superintendent wasn't very well liked by any of the workers. That's putting it mildly. They thought he was the lowest, sneakiest, and generally the orneriest person they had ever seen. The other supervisors and foremen didn't like him much either. So the only friend he had in the plant was 'the boss man,' and 'the boss man' made it pretty clear he wanted him to keep his distance and do his job and that was about all. Well, that left this superintendent without any friends at all and while he was at work he was a pretty unhappy fellow, although I guess he would have been the last in the world to admit it. I happen to know that his unhappiness at work affected his home life around that time too. He tried to be the same bullheaded guy there as he was around the plant, and he let a lot of ill feeling built up at work out on his wife and kids. As a result the family situation was pretty rough and the youngster was growing up in an unpleasant home.

"Then came 1932 and Charlie McCormick set up this Multiple Management. As part of it, he established a Junior Board, and later a Factory Board and a Sales Board. He appointed the first members, but every six months ever since then the members are selected by the men on the boards themselves by a merit rating system. Well, sir, he appointed this plant superintendent I've been telling you about to the first Factory Board. He explained to me later that he thought he understood people, and he could see that this fellow had a fine technical knowledge of everything down in the plant and basically was a good person who had got off the track somehow on dealing with people. He had grown so warped under the old system in Mr. Willoughby's day that he never had a

chance to become a human being. So Charlie put him on the original Factory Board along with supervisors and fellows from different levels all through the plant. The board went to work having meetings regularly to talk about things they thought ought to be improved around the place and make recommendations to the Senior Board of Directors for action on them.

"Well, that superintendent fitted into that picture just about like you would expect. Even in the board meetings where everybody was supposed to be on the same basis, he couldn't get over the idea that he was top dog as plant superintendent and he tried to ride roughshod over everyone. When some pretty hot arguments occurred, this fellow just tried to dominate the board instead of working matters out on a co-operative basis as the board was supposed to do.

"When the time came for the Factory Board members to rate their fellow members to see who was going to serve on the board for the next six months' term, they did an honest job on this plant superintendent and really rated him down where he belonged on things like co-operativeness, attitude, and dealing with people. Even though he ranked pretty high on efficiency and things like that, the other poor ratings brought him so low that he was dropped from the board as one of the bottom three in the rating.

"Well, this 'super' hit the ceiling. He told 'em off good, and then the Factory Board executive committee fellows decided to tell him why they had rated him like they did. They repeated everything that people around the place had been saying about him for years and at the end they summed it up in one sentence which was sure right and reflected what everybody thought: 'You know your production, but everybody thinks you are just an ornery, sneaky, double-crossing son of a so-and-so!'

"Boy, that superintendent was some mad! He stormed up to Charlie McCormick and started right in: 'Well, they kicked me off the Factory Board. I guess I'm through. I'll pick up my salary by mail if it's all right with you,'

"Charlie McCormick looked at this man and said: 'You mean you're quitting?'

"The super was a little upset when he heard that. 'Quitting?' he said. 'Why, I don't know if I'm quitting or not, but they kicked me off the Factory Board and if I'm not on the board how could I be plant superintendent?' 'Yes,' said Charlie McCormick, 'I know they kicked you off the board. I'll bet I can guess what they said to you when they did it too. They probably said you were a good plant superintendent when it came to production and efficiency and ability, but that you were so stubborn and mean about handling people that they just couldn't put up with you any longer. Is that right?'

"The super said yes, that was so.

" 'Well, as a matter of fact,' said Charlie, 'they are mostly right, but that doesn't mean that you have to give up your job as superintendent. That's up to you. You know now what your fellow workers think about you, and you've got it straight from them for the first time. The real question is whether your own opinion of yourself is right, or whether you are big enough to be able to listen to others and try to do something about it. Now, if you want your job it's still here. Take a day off or a week off, or whatever time you want, get yourself adjusted, and then come back and see if you can't change your ways, treat people like human beings and be a human being yourself. Okay?'

"The superintendent stood there a minute and then he turned around and walked out. I guess he was a pretty confused guy. After being with the company for so many years he didn't want to leave. He was making a good salary. As a matter of fact he didn't know right then where to go for another job. Most important of all, I guess he had a suspicion that maybe there was something to what the people on the Factory Board had said about him.

"Well, I wish I could say that this guy walked in next day as a changed man, but that wouldn't be the truth. It took him a long time to change—over a year. He stayed on as plant superintendent. He thought a lot about what had happened, and he worked at trying to do something about it. He still had the same technical knowledge and the same efficiency, and he began to improve a little as time went on about getting along with people.

"I don't know just when the turning point really came, but anyway this superintendent improved enough that everybody began to see that he was not the same guy he used to be. And then one day the Factory Board told him that he had been rerated and that he was going to get a chance to come back for a six months' term.

"This time he did better; he didn't try to run everything his way, and he was willing to listen and take part with the others in the suggestions that went through. He began to see that you could co-operate with people and still keep your authority and efficiency. He began to have a regard for the other fellow's opinions. He got to be a lot better as a human being.

"If you come down to one of our company dinners some night these days—like when the Senior, Junior, and Factory Boards get together—you'll see this fellow. He'll be in the background, but he'll have charge of seeing that the dinner is served just right. It's a hobby he picked up along with his regular work in the plant. He really doesn't have to come in until 8:30 in the morning, but he's downtown every morning around seven o'clock—not at the office, but up the street *about three blocks away at the open-air vegetable markets. You see, our new plant cafeteria for the employees was built in 1936 and this fellow found that he got a big kick out of trying to make it the best cafeteria around. So he comes down to do the buying of the fresh vegetables personally, then goes to work on his regular job.*

"I could tell you a lot more about this fellow—about his happy home life now and about the joy he is getting out of life now. But the main point I want to make is this—here's what we are really talking about when we talk about good human relations, here is the kind of thing it does.

"If you want to see the factory's production record under Multiple Management we can show you that, and it's a good picture too. But, most important, if you want to see what it does for people, you have to look into the lives of everyone here in this place, look into their lives not just as workers but as people, as the members of families and, most of all, as human beings.

"Oh, yes, I ought to tell you too that this fellow who was kicked off the first Factory Board not only came back on the board but since then he has been elected chairman six times.

"Well, I guess I should tell you—it's no secret to anyone here at McCormick & Company. You are probably wondering how I know so much about this man. Well, I should. You know who he is? It was me. . . . Yessir, by God, it was me."

CHAPTER I

BUSINESS IS PEOPLE

THE president of a business is a trustee for all the people who work in it. When he assumes the job, he takes on the responsibility of making a profit, first of all. He owes that obligation to the stockholders and also to all who depend for jobs on the success of the business. It is my opinion he'll fulfill his function of profit-making best if he always remembers his obligations not only to the stockholders but also to his employees and to the consuming public as well.

Many labor unions exist today because in the past management has failed to look after the welfare of its workers. When any segment of society offends the essential human dignity of the people who make their living in a business enterprise, when power becomes so great that the rights of individuals are subordinated to dictatorial authority, then the will of the people asserts itself and there is a change. Management *has* been guilty of abusing its power. I think that today the tables are being turned. The sins of omission that heretofore were practiced by management and led to the formation of labor unions, today threaten to become constricting to certain labor unions.

My greatest satisfaction as president of a company has been in watching people who work with me grow as the business grows. The employee who was speaking to you on the previous pages is not a mythical Mr. Smith, but a flesh-and-blood man here in our company whose words were taken verbatim from a recording machine. I think the experience of this

1

factory superintendent is important to America and to the world. This story and others like it give all of us a hope and a challenge for the future that is strengthened by faith.

I believe in these principles with deep conviction:

1. Business is primarily a matter of people. Men, not machines alone, have brought the United States to its dominant position in world industry. The machines would never be here if men had not inspired and used their minds and energies toward making these great contributions to mankind. No machine was ever invented that performed any useful function until people operated it and managed it.

2. Employees are human beings first, citizens of our nation second, and factors in production third. Labor is not a commodity to be bought, sold, or exchanged in the market place. Labor can never be really understood if considered solely in the mass. The great working force of any business is a collection of individual human beings, all with individual rights and individual problems worthy of consideration by management and government.

3. The United States is the bulwark of individual freedom and economic stability in the world today. Its greatness, its abundance, and its wealth place upon us the greatest challenge and at the same time the greatest opportunity ever known. There are definite signs of our realizing our responsibility.

4. The welfare of the people cannot be legislated satisfactorily by any government. Laws may regulate and control, but only free management and free labor, working co-operatively within the framework of our society, can initiate and maintain the long-range striving for the public good that is the aim of democracy. The government must always be impartial and just to all factions if it is to maintain the best for all groups.

5. The ability of American business managers acting jointly with American workers to preserve the "dignity of man" and "freedom of choice" for the individual is the only positive approach toward obtaining and preserving democracy throughout the world. We need human relations leaders. Our oncoming generation has a real opportunity to capitalize on our good start.

6. Finally, the destiny of man lies in being of service to others. No government or philosophy has ever lastingly endured unless it was

based on a "religious" or "service" motive for bettering mankind. No man, however rich or powerful, can make his proper contribution to society unless his life is built around serving others. We were placed here to improve the society in which we live and that should be the goal of business and professional leaders today, tomorrow, and forever.

The recognition of the importance of the individual goes all the way back to the ancient Greeks. They formulated a basic rule of life which, like most great truths, is essentially simple, consisting of two words: "Know Thyself." Several centuries later a poet named Alexander Pope put a new twist on this truth. Said he: "The proper study of mankind is man."

But the world sidetracked most of the wisdom of philosophers and rushed down the heady scientific paths of facts. The measurement of things, not the study of man, became the order of the day. The path was a long and pleasant one, with new machines, the wonders of electricity and electronics, new medicines, new comforts, and new luxuries heightening the pace of life and man's enjoyment of it. Science was outstripping the human development of society.

However, the time has come now that we must catch up with science by expanding our knowledge of the social sciences that lead to the improvement of human relations among men. Eric Johnston, whose practical vision and keen insight I value highly, has put it all into one terse sentence: "Mechanically, we are traveling in America at the speed of a jet plane; socially, we are still plodding along at the pace of an ox cart."

The scientists recognize the problem too. The same men who invented the atomic bomb now spend their days and nights in translating their discovery into terms of usefulness as a source of peaceful power. Many of them who would much prefer the quiet of their laboratories to the public rostrum have taken to the speaking stand or to the printed page to urge the proper control of atomic energy and to warn mankind, who might otherwise misuse it, of the immeasurably potent force they have created.

"Man's control over the material world has grown to be far greater than his mastery of himself. Man, not matter, is the chief problem of the world today," said Edmond W. Sinnott recently. Mr. Sinnott is not a preacher. He is dean of the Sheffield Scientific School at Yale University.

Men, not machines or material objects, should be the chief subject of our future study and research. Through God, this is a man-made world. What man makes, surely man must be able to control. Wars, depressions, poverty, and strife between groups can all be solved ultimately if we will only bring our enormous powers of research to bear upon these pressing problems. The next generation will have a great opportunity to solve many of these problems, and I am sure it will.

Perhaps you are beginning to wonder how all this concerns business. It has everything to do with business. As management executives, we deal not only with buying and selling, with economic trends and profits, but also with men and women. We who are trustees or employees of business as a management team are in the best possible position to lead in the study and the steady development of individual human beings.

Of course you realize that every man who works for a living spends half his waking hours on the job. Assuming that eight hours of every calendar day are devoted to sleep, and eight hours to work, we can truthfully say that half a man's existence is bound up in his working hours. Because of this fact business is and should be the most powerful influence in America and in the world. It has not only the greatest potential for good, but also the greatest responsibility to function in the public interest. Accordingly, business, far from being complacent, must be increasingly self-analytical and self-improving.

Business systems should be built around the fundamental cravings, desires, and needs of human nature. Within this framework, all strife between groups can be resolved eventually. The problems we know in the United States between labor and management and the controversy between free competitive business enterprise and socialistic ownership of basic industry by government can be solved by determining what people want and making sure their welfare as well as the good of the enterprise is considered. Communism need not loom as a menace if the "dignity of man" is remembered. Our humanized capitalistic system can triumph easily if its leaders remember to serve mankind and respect the individual rights of all men.

I am convinced that the job must begin here at home—in each individual business. I would rather see free business management take the initiative to meet the needs of human nature and win the credit for so doing than to see us coerced eventually, if we fail to do so, by law or by organized pressure of aroused partisan groups.

What are the things, then, that man as an employee asks of the job that occupies him for half his waking life? What are the factors that the instincts of human nature lead him to expect and to want? If these can be determined by business management, and then supplied by progressive action, we can solve more than the long-run problems of survival of a system. We solve at the same time the short-range question of higher productivity, reduced costs, and continuing profits to keep the business alive, for in meeting the needs of human nature we stimulate in employees not only their loyalty to a system but at the same time their increased interest and effort in the company for which they work. Increased production definitely is the key to the door of higher living standards.

It is impossible continuously to drive people for any length of time to do a better job. People cannot be coerced—they can only be led through the contentment they find in their work. I was shocked to learn from a recent nation-wide survey of factory workers that more than half the workers who were asked to state their opinion of their jobs said flatly they did not like their jobs and stayed on them only because the pay they received supplied sufficient incentive for them to put up with the irksomeness of their work. Production is affected by the attitude of the worker toward his job. Increased productivity can be guaranteed through happy employees.

Our study of people as employees, therefore, should go back first to a determination of the things innate in human nature that make people enjoy their work and lead them to be more productive for their own interests.

I think there are only five basic factors that employees want from their jobs:

1. Fair pay. Money is not everything, but it is, of course, important and may be placed first in the list of the things employees want. Note that I have used the word "fair" rather than the word "good." I am convinced that employee satisfaction depends as much on the worker's feeling that he is being paid fairly and without discrimination in relation to other employees of similar skills as it does on the actual amount of the pay envelope. Only careful attention to the right job classifications and right wages can assure this fairness. Management cannot be just unless it knows these factors and studies them constantly.

2. Security. As a man grows older, his hourly rate of pay becomes less important than his instinctive human desire for security of income over a long-range period. As I analyze it, there are three distinct types of security, which every business management executive must keep in mind constantly—security by the *day*, which involves consideration of what happens to a man's income if he becomes ill and must miss a day or several days of work; security by the *year*, which raises the question of subjection to layoffs and the feeling in

the worker's mind that he should have a steady job and a steady income to count on throughout the year; and finally, security for *life*, which brings in the question of retirement pensions and other measures that give some assurance to a worker of subsistence income when he becomes too old to work actively. If management is to remain the leader, then it must lead in the solution of these problems.

3. Opportunity. To the young man, opportunity is an even more significant factor of human nature than security. He wants to know what his chances are to advance if he does his work well, what the possibilities are of increasing his income and his position as he gains in experience and skill. He likes to be respected in his society, too. Particularly for the creative and ambitious type of worker, the question of opportunity and future potential may even surpass the question of hourly pay or weekly salary. Systematic merit upgrading plans and promotion systems are effective attempts to answer this basic craving for opportunity. Private enterprise gives opportunity and partial security—communism offers only a false security to workers.

4. Recognition. This costs relatively little, but is used poorly by many management executives. I wonder sometimes how it can be overlooked so completely. When American workers were asked to write to the *Reader's Digest* and state their views on the question "What's Wrong With Management?" the great majority of the replies had nothing whatsoever to say about pay, or security, or benefits. By far the greater number of letters made the point in different words: "We want to be treated like human beings by management, and we want to be recognized as such." The pat on the back for a job well done, the evidence of interest on the part of supervisors and foremen and even top executives when a worker or a department carries out an assignment well, the systematic singling out of workers by public recognition of points of excellence—all are factors in the worker's mind which are essential to job satisfaction.

At McCormick & Company, we have departed from the haphazard granting of recognition whenever a foreman happens to think about it or feels right after a good breakfast, and have replaced this customary hit-or-miss operation of the recognition factor by a planned system. We give President's Awards publicly at employee meetings to employees who have either done a consistently good job for a period of time or who have shown outstanding ability or interest on a short or long-range project, and for unusual traits of character.

We naturally have Service Awards for length of service. However, a recognition system is not complete unless it includes recognition for merit as well as for the mere fact of having been around for a number of years. How important to the human being is the eagle on the colonel's shoulder, the broad stripe of the admiral on his sleeve, and the pins worn by men on their lapel? Recognition by the public is vanity but also a deep desire of man. Why not use these forces—to advantage.

5. Participation. Any study of man as a human being will reveal a fundamental desire of human nature which most business managements forget. One of our basic needs is to be a part of a group. We join churches, we join clubs, we join lodges; we may join labor unions because we seek the sympathetic companionship of our fellow men and want to join others on matters of common interest. Business management would do well to examine carefully this proved craving of human nature. Employees would like to feel they are a part of a business too, not just a number on the payroll. They would like to have some way of expressing themselves. They would like to communicate what they feel and what they believe not only to an immediate foreman or supervisor, but often to the front office. They would like to be brought together by management, in meetings and groups where information would be given to them so that they could feel they were a part of the business. They like to be acquainted with their business and its problems. If they are "thinkers," they like to share in the planning of working policies and establishment of practices in such a way that the creative and ambitious ones among them would be given some process through which to express their minds. Many may not feel that management has extended the right of participation when it deals with their labor union. They often feel instead, perhaps rightfully, that their labor union has won for them the right to such participation and give management no credit for the accomplishment. At McCormick & Company we have pioneered on this question of participation more than on any other factor among the five I have listed here. Herein lies what I believe to be our real contribution to the science of better human relations and

consideration for people. We have found a way for people to participate—in group or council meetings, in management boards through which the most creative and ambitious future executive type of employees offer their ideas for the good of the entire company, and even through sharing of the profit with all employees who have helped to earn the profits through their co-operative endeavor. No man can take full credit for everything he has done. Others are a part of our success, and private enterprise can be at its best only if all feel that way about it and are proportionately rewarded according to their contribution. We owe our ancestors much and our followers even more.

For seventeen years at McCormick's we have carefully experimented with the problems of human relations. We have now gone past the research stage. Our experience, and that of nearly a thousand other firms which have adapted some of our methods, has shown that our work on human relations can no longer be considered either a theory or a laboratory test but rather a tested and proved workable program. We propose to tell how we have attempted to fulfill the basic needs of human nature in the chapters that follow on "Multiple Management."

CHAPTER II

A NEW HUMAN RELATIONS
PHILOSOPHY

McCORMICK & COMPANY was founded in 1889 by my uncle, Willoughby M. McCormick. He started in business in Baltimore with a line of spices and extracts, which he mixed and sold, with the help of only two assistants, in a tiny one-room plant. The truth of his original slogan, "Make the best—someone will buy it," was proved by the company's metamorphosis into a multimillion-dollar business.

But though sales hit the five million mark in 1928, my uncle still ruled with as firm a hand as he had in the one-room factory. Three times a day he made a tour of inspection to see for himself that everyone was hustling on the job. What he didn't know was that his path was heralded by warning signals and that after he passed the workers relaxed. When it came to taking advice from others, my uncle was likewise an industrialist of the old school. He behaved like a proud father who was loath to believe that his children could grow up. He resented what he considered "impertinent attempts at interference" from well-meaning employees and supervisors and his only too plainly expressed attitude could be summed up: "You do your jobs and I'll make the decisions." As a result of his authoritative manner, as well as thrice-yearly seasonal layoffs and other poor employment practices, employee morale was low.

Since my uncle had no children and there was a possibility

that someday I might fill his place, he took me into the company during my summer vacations. After I left college, he put me through an intensive course of training. From 1915 to 1932, with time out for a two-year stretch in the Navy, I worked my way up from handling freight on the shipping platform to operating machines in the factory to a special course in the offices, which was followed by selling merchandise all over the country and abroad.

From time to time, I thought of ways to improve the management of the business and in my first few years at McCormick I relayed these ideas to my uncle. He listened patiently and with a peculiar smile, but seldom acted upon any of these suggestions. Finally one day he informed me, in blunt and unmistakable terms, that he alone was the sole management of McCormick. I do not blame my uncle. He was right from his point of view. He was of a generation that believed in keeping youth in its place.

After the stock market crash of 1929, McCormick & Company, like many other firms, was hard hit. In 1932 my uncle told the Board of Directors that a further cut in wages would be necessary if the company was to stay in business. Shortly afterward he died.

At that unpropitious time, ninety days before President Franklin D. Roosevelt closed the banks, I was elected by the board to the presidency of the company. Immediately I decided to test some of my theories on human relations. The board called an employee meeting and made what was a highly unusual proposal for the times. It would cut the work week from 56 hours to 45 hours and not lower wages, but raise them 10 per cent. The only way the company could survive under this schedule was to boost production, since then it could lower costs, reduce prices, and increase its sales. We made it plain that from now on the workers would prosper if the company prospered. The workers responded by raising output so much that, partly as a result of higher production and partly from other multiple management policies, in a year the company's finances changed from the red to the black.

At the same time I was looking for a way to stimulate the thinking of McCormick's executives. Somewhere I had read that the average businessman utilizes only about half of his mental capacity. I wanted to find methods of lifting our men out of the routine ruts that suppress imagination and inventiveness. The solution came to me at the next meeting of the Board of Directors. Glancing around, I realized that while I was thirty-six years old, nearly all the members were over forty-five and several had passed sixty. Through long years of discipline, they had acquired the habit of automatically yessing my uncle's judgment. While all subjects of importance were brought up at board meetings, the final decisions invariably rested with Willoughby McCormick, who was in a position to know more about the business than anyone else and could argue down any opposition.

I had taken stock of myself and had arrived at the conviction that I possessed neither the ability nor the inclination to be a one-man manager of a multimillion-dollar business. I told the directors that I appreciated the value of their individual experience, mature judgment, and collective wisdom, but thought we should exhaust every source of ideas and information. To accomplish this, I suggested the formation of a Junior Board of Directors, to be chosen from among assistant department managers and others who had shown special zeal in their work. The purpose of the Junior Board then, as it is now, would be not to by-pass the judgment of the more mature men, but to supplement that judgment with new ideas.

The original seventeen-man Junior Board was appointed by me; since then, the Junior Board members themselves have held the elections. From the start, the board elected its own officers, wrote its own constitution and bylaws and governed itself without outside interference. The only checks upon it were that all proposals had to be passed unanimously before any action could be taken and that all major suggestions had to be sent to the Senior Board for approval. Because I wanted to give the young men a chance to advance in the company, I promised that henceforth all members of the Senior Board of Directors would be recruited from the ranks of the Junior Board.

Thus was Multiple Management born.

Today Multiple Management is not an idealist's dream but a practical scheme functioning in a company which employs about 1,500 people and operates on an international scale. Our products—spices, flavoring extracts, teas, condiments, dehydrated foods, food colors, household and garden insecticides, soluble fertilizers, and drugs—are prepared from formulae developed in our own research laboratory or experimental farm and greenhouses. They are manufactured through intricate, high-speed production methods, then are packed and sold at plants and warehouses in Baltimore, New York, San Francisco, Memphis, Houston, and Mexico City. A crew of 350 salesmen markets the wares to wholesale distributors, supermarkets, institutions, and retail stores. The business is complex, both from the supply end, because raw materials come from many foreign countries, and from the sales end, since the goods are sold all over the world through the McCormick Overseas Trading Company, Inc. Because the market is highly competitive, McCormick advertises extensively in newspapers, national magazines, and on the radio.

In 1947 we acquired A. Schilling & Company of San Francisco, a big spice house on the West Coast. The merger was widely discussed because it didn't displace a single Schilling employee and the Schilling management remained intact just as it was before.

Multiple Management can work in either a union or a non-union shop. The Schilling division deals with several national unions, yet Multiple Management is being introduced successfully. The Baltimore division of McCormick & Company has always been an open shop. We have never resisted or in any way disapproved the entry or formation of unions. Back in 1938 a union organizer appeared and announced his intention of organizing a national union in our plant. I welcomed him into my office and made the following proposal:

"How would it be," I started, "if we approached the topic in this manner? Here are two cigars. I'll light up and smoke mine while you talk. Then you sit back, puffing on yours, while I talk. All right?"

My visitor agreed and the conference began. We both made our points clearly, without pulling any punches. At the end of an hour the union organizer rose and reached for his hat.

"Mr. McCormick," he said, "I think there are a lot of other plants that need organizing more than yours does."

I assured him that we weren't perfect, and he was welcome to try to organize our people if he so desired.

"No, I don't think it would make much sense," he said slowly.

He walked toward the door, then turned back as though struck by a sudden thought.

"As a matter of fact, I'll tell you something. If all companies regarded their employees as you people do here, I'd soon be out of a job. God bless you. Why don't you write a book about it so people will know what you are doing in human relations?"

CHAPTER III

MULTIPLE MANAGEMENT IN ACTION

HERE at McCormick & Company we supplement the regular line organization with Multiple Management. Major policy changes proposed under Multiple Management are put into effect and are carried out by the line organization after being approved by the Senior Board of Directors. This board is selected by the stockholders annually, with no limit on re-election.

The Multiple Management plan is built on a firm concept of putting people first. The plan operates through a combination of auxiliary management boards, participation, sponsorship, merit rating, and two-way communication between all employees and management. A major aim is to eliminate one-man rule in business and to train and develop young executives in accordance with their merit, rather than their age. The real secret of its success is participation; it offers administrative outlets for our basic needs as workers.

Multiple Management is a democratic method of government for business. The active management is carried on through groups of more than fifty persons instead of a few executive officers. These groups are: (1) the Factory Board; (2) the Sales Board; (3) the Junior Board; (4) the Institutional Sales Board; (5) the Senior Board.

The members of the Junior and Factory Boards are chosen by board members themselves at elections held semiannually.

15

Elections are by ballot, using a rating system, so selection is by merit and not popularity.

Members of the Sales Board represent both the inside sales, advertising and merchandising departments, and men outside actively engaged in the field. The members from the Baltimore office are appointed by the Senior Board, and the outside members are elected by ballot for a period of one year, according to their accomplishments during the past year.

As I said, the Senior Board is elected by the stockholders. Since 1932 new members elected to the Board of Directors have, with one exception, all been men who previously served on one of the other Boards.

The Factory Board represents factory employees. Its problems concern factory management—working conditions, employees' suggestions, etc., and improving the relationship between the company and its employees.

The Sales Board is composed of fifteen men active in sales positions. These men are both those actively engaged in outside selling as well as sales executives in the Baltimore office.

The Junior Board represents the office employees and those concerned with personnel and administration. Its problems are chiefly those of administration or direction, personnel and office management.

All suggestions of the subordinate boards must be approved unanimously before being forwarded to the Senior Board. The Senior Board, in its turn, must give unanimous approval before the suggestions are passed along to the line organization for action. This ruling is insurance against the violent splits of opinion often found in such boards. Furthermore, it tends to tone down the wilder ideas. Those interested in specific bylaws governing the various boards will find these in Appendix B to E of this book.

In my opinion each company should examine its own needs, then adopt and adapt the basic Multiple Management concept best suited to those needs.

I want to make it clear that our board posts are not in any sense merely honorary. Each member is paid extra fees for the time spent on board business. He is given to understand that his board has a job to do and responsibilities to fulfill. This is vital. Any company which attempts to install Multiple Management in a halfhearted manner will find its purpose defeated. Every man on the board must be convinced of the importance of the board's functions, as well as the need for his own best efforts to that end. To achieve this, we see that all major company decisions pass through the board concerned.

CHAPTER IV

WHY MULTIPLE MANAGEMENT WORKS

BEFORE going further into the inception and operation of the Junior, Factory, and Sales Boards, let me examine the social and psychological factors involved in the board aspects of Multiple Management. There are certain obvious advantages in the board plan. It brings new blood into the managerial structure. It constitutes a form of recognition and promotion in addition to normal channels. It stimulates new interest in every department of the company, makes our people feel that they have careers and that they belong to the enterprise rather than that they just hold down ordinary jobs. It enables us to train employees to study the business and take on responsibility as rapidly as they are able. Rewarding all workers on a basis of merit, rather than favoritism or "popularity," convinces them that when they improve the business in any way they are advancing themselves as well.

But more important than any of these, it actually produces more mature men and women. Now, "maturity" can mean many things; some people mistake dogmatism for maturity. People who "know their own minds" at an early age are often called mature. Actually, such people are largely unthinking, they have simply closed their minds to new and progressive ideas. Maturity, as I see it, is the ability to keep an open mind, be tolerant, and understand people, to accept opinions other than your own, to give the other man credit when credit is due.

A few months ago I read a description of how the first United States Atomic Energy Committee went about writing its historic policy report. Here were gathered men from various walks of life, men of character, wisdom, executive ability, and great responsibility. They realized the enormity of their task. In their sole possession was the greatest weapon for good or evil the world has ever known. What should be the policy, before our own people and the world? These five men decided on a unique approach.

They were supposed to function as a committee. They knew what their objective was—the shaping of a policy that could steer future United States atomic energy development and control through the stormy days of war and peace that lay ahead. What did these men do? Did they sit down around a table and plunge into their task? No. At their first meetings they decided something like this:

"This is probably one of the most important committees ever appointed. We Americans dote on the committee system. Whenever we have a problem or a job to do, we shape it up around a committee. This attitude probably stems from our inherent dislike of one-man rule. But many committees fail to handle the jobs assigned them. The members get into arguments. Factions form. People choose sides and defend, rather than explore. Too many committee reports end up in wishy-washy compromise form; ineffectual and inconclusive. Therefore, if we are to function efficiently as a committee, let us first undertake to study why some committees fail, and how we can avoid such traps."

So this all-important committee started out to study committee behavior. Finally, they decided that three things usually hampered committee work. First, faulty communication. Members of committees often got into hot arguments over ideas and terms, without really understanding what the other side was arguing about. They heard each other very well, but they didn't understand each other at all. Conceptual words like "democracy," often meant three different things to three different persons. Therefore, the Atomic Energy Committeemen decided that they would all take pains to define the terms to be discussed.

Second, they found that many committees fell apart because their members came, not to examine facts and look for truth, but to defend preconceived viewpoints. Therefore, the members of this committee resolved to attempt to "liberate themselves from the tyranny of their own egos" and to be logical and objective, rather than emotional and subjective, in approaching all proposals.

Finally, to avoid issuing a watered-down, ineffectual compromise statement, they decided that all conclusions must be reached through unanimous agreement.

The story of this committee's deliberations and findings, and how agreement was finally reached after an apparent unresolvable deadlock, is one of truly historic importance which may be read elsewhere in full. But the committee's reasoning in approaching its task was exciting to me, for it revealed the inherent soundness of the approach we had followed in our board system for over fifteen years. Without exercising the same theoretical, scientific approach, we had established a working procedure which allowed us to avoid the very pitfalls the Atomic Energy Committee warned against. And in doing so, we had established a firm core of mature people; people who could bring to fulfillment the human relations objectives we were moving toward.

The most important accomplishment of the board system is its ability to inculcate respect for the other fellow's opinion. You can preach understanding, respect, and tolerance until the cows come home, but it won't get across until people realize themselves; until they feel it. The board system throws together people from all types of background, young and old, college men and grammar school graduates, accountants and salesmen. We insist on mutual respect. Every man gets a hearing. And there are few meetings at which a sound and ingenious idea doesn't spring from an unexpected source. After witnessing this for a few months, and having some of his own ideas examined under a critical group microscope, it's a rare board member who doesn't feel less cocksure of his own infallibility. And it's natural that this respect for others should carry over into his day-to-day attitude in the plant. Once the worker feels that his foreman or department head has an innate respect for his ideas, the rest follows. We have the beginning of that atmosphere of security which is so important to successful human relations.

Another contribution of great value is the ability of the board system to break down the restricting barriers of departmental interest common to many businesses. Certainly it is axiomatic that any integrated business must function as an organic whole. But we are all familiar with companies that are split by internal departmental feuds and jealousies. The shipping men have an undeclared war with the production department, and the advertising group is always being sabotaged by the printers. The maintenance men feel that no one understands their problems, and everyone causes them unnecessary work and hardship. And so it goes. Instead of functioning as a team, we see such companies run as a score of separate units, all pulling in different directions. Often this stems from the department heads and even top management. Since the emphasis is on specialization, these men often have little idea of other departments' needs or the operation of the business as a whole.

The board system brings together men from all departments. In exploring the various problems involved, each man gets an excellent grounding in the needs and objectives of departments other than his own. He sees clearly the importance of teamwork, of co-ordinating his department's work into the entire flow of purchasing, storage, production, sales, distribution, and administration. And he finds that the other people often have ideas and suggestions that are invaluable in solving his problem.

I should like to emphasize here our belief in the value of transferals. Our people are hired not alone for a specific job, but for a McCormick job. If work slackens or piles up in one department, workers are shifted to compensate. Their desires are given every consideration. Workers desiring to transfer to other departments are allowed to do so whenever openings occur; many times mutual swaps are made. Production teams trade jobs on an hourly or daily basis; we find that all such arrangements help eliminate work fatigue brought on by monotony. Further, they produce a wealth of ingenious suggestions for improvements in various departments. We carry out this philosophy on all levels; several of our crack salesmen were ranking executives in accounting or production work who desired a change. We know from experience that loyalty and enthusiasm are splendid catalysts in job performance and we do everything possible to develop these precious qualities.

If sound human relations is the heart of our managerial structure, then merit rating may be called its lifeblood. All members of the Junior and Factory Boards are elected by vote of the board members themselves, at a merit rating session held once every six months. (Every McCormick employee is rated every six months after becoming a regular employee, or he may request a rating at any other time if he feels his job and rate of pay are not commensurate with his abilities. But since we are now concerned with board administration, I shall discuss only that specific phase of merit rating here.)

We continually attempt to impress upon board members that merit rating must be based on actual executive potentialities, not popularity. The board should attempt to reward neither an occasional flash of genius nor service distinguished only by longevity and good intent. To ensure objectivity as much as possible, we have worked out the rating chart shown in Appendix A.

Some might think that the boards degenerate into a fixed, self-perpetuating group. Nothing could be further from the truth. Our men have been as objective as an adding machine in making their appraisals. Mere popularity or friendship has never been enough to win a man a permanent post. The board members rightly regard their jobs as a form of trusteeship for the entire McCormick work force, and they feel it would be a breach of that confidence to have "deadheads" in the group. Looking back over the old merit rating slips, I note several instances where members have been voted off the boards for being yes men, for "lack of constructive thinking," and such weaknesses. The maintenance of such high standards not only ensures peak board caliber, it also justifies the entire merit rating system used throughout the plant. Employees have less resentment against merit rating when they know that management also is required to toe the mark.

New board membership and executive or administrative talent is efficiently surveyed by our sponsorship system. Like many other offspring of Multiple Management, the sponsorship idea has spread widely since we began to use it in the early thirties. Reduced to its simplest form, the sponsorship plan attempts to give every thinking or creative newcomer a close, personal contact in the company; someone who can answer his questions. We put an added twist to this formula by having sponsors on the executive and administrative levels appraise the talents, character, and personalities of the new men in terms of future managerial capabilities. This appraisal is by no means the only or final one, but it enables us to begin working with the newcomer early in the game, on an informal, intimate basis.

There is one good characteristic common in most of the young men who start with us—they want to do a lot of thinking for themselves, to try their mental spurs. Some are timid; others are cocksure and aggressive; some are obviously suffering with inferiority complexes, while a few are just as surely egotistical; but within a few weeks all who remain with us express a certain spirit of independence. The newcomer finds that he can express himself without the return of ridicule, and that what he says is considered respectfully even when he is wrong. Also, he finds that he can govern his own activities within reasonable limits. Every effort is made to avoid suppressing his enthusiasm and demoralizing his ambition and initiative.

This course might be ill-advised or even disastrous in many cases, if the newcomers were not governed by their sponsors and the Junior Board. After some time, as the apprentice progresses, he is likely to think of a different way to do his work, and he may consider the established proceedings to be all wrong. He speaks to his sponsor about it, and if the idea is worthless, as it usually is, the more experienced man is careful to prove its fallacies without discouraging him. If the idea seems to be practicable, he is informed by his sponsor that changes are never made without the authorization of the Junior Board and that his suggested idea will be discussed and possibly approved at the next meeting.

This does not in any way detract from the authority of the managers of departments over the young employees. The manager always knows what is going on and who in his department is making progress. If a new man goes to him with a suggestion that seems to be worth while, he will tell him that the plan must go to the Junior Board for discussion and approval, explaining that sixteen judges are better than one, and that discussion may bring out ways of improving and applying the idea.

In this way each apprentice is encouraged to respect sound authority. He is counseled and guided, as well as governed, by men whom he respects because they have the knowledge and experience he wants, and because they are of his own generation. They can say anything they think is right to him and he will take it and think it over seriously, whereas if one of us old executives said the same thing in the same way it might serve to congeal his mind and detour his thinking with suppressed anger and resentment. Coddling of youngsters in business is always either demoralizing or disastrous. Frequently, it results when such authority is placed in the hands of men so old that they have forgotten their own youth. The young men who make up our Junior Board of Executives vividly remember the vagaries, activities, and ambitions of their youth; they remember, also, the rules of sportsmanship; and in the experience of our company they have made sponsoring a necessary factor in building men to build the business.

Some of the boys who start with us apparently expect to find their entrance into business life a rather dull adventure. They are pleasantly surprised to find it otherwise. If they have not been to college, it is a new experience for them. If they are university graduates, they are reminded of the principles of their athletic training and contests, and something of their fraternity associations. They are led to understand the elements of good sportsmanship in business.

To old-time executives this may seem like impractical college bunk. They may believe that when a man leaves high school or college it is best for him to forget the past and face the hard, cold facts of business. But I notice that hard-boiled businessmen in large flocks pay their four dollars and forty cents a head to give vent to their enthusiasm on Saturday afternoons at football games. I also notice that the hard-boiled business fathers of the playing youngsters are the most enthusiastic rooters in the stands.

There must be something basically fine and valuable in the spirit fostered by good college athletics and fraternities to attract so much favorable attention when it is manifested on the playing field. Again, there must be something fine and valuable in anything that will hold the loyalty and pride of men all through the years of their lives. It is my contention that these values should not be lost in the transition from the campus to business. We endeavor to preserve and organize these values, especially for the benefit of its people who have not had the advantages of college training and for its factory workers.

All businessmen, I think, realize the supreme value of loyalty throughout an organization. I have heard many discussions of the subject, mainly in the form of complaints regarding the lack of loyalty. I have listened to many pep talks that considered loyalty as a sort of duty that should be delivered in return for every pay check and envelope. But loyalty is too precious a thing to be bought and paid for; it must be earned with service that is sincere and just and generous. Therefore, the primary and everlasting purpose of management should be to build every division of its business in ways that will be deserving and worthy of the loyalty of all the people it employs. This, in the highest sense, is consideration of the human factor in business.

We believe that almost nothing is as important to individual development as successful job placement. We spend constant time and money in attempting to avoid placing a round peg in a square hole, and vice versa. Moreover, we try to avoid getting "fixes" on people, a common failing among some supervisors. By this I mean their tendency to size up a person early in the game, and then relegate him to one particular type of job. We know from experience that the human potential constantly changes. A listless young man may become a veritable human dynamo after marriage and the arrival of his first child. The clearing up of a family problem may release a new torrent of productive energy in a worker. Or a movie he may see, a book he may have read—these and many other catalysts can work amazing changes in a man's attitudes and talents. We believe it fatal to stifle a twenty-talent man in a ten-talent job. But we also believe it fatal to place a twenty-talent man in a thirty-talent job. So we strive constantly, through all supervisory levels, to appraise accurately and promote or demote accordingly. But always we make such moves after talking them over with the people involved, making sure they are aware of the reasons involved.

Our sponsorship plan is closely allied to a firm policy of promoting from within. Nothing is more devastating to worker morale than a constant influx of outsiders into desirable jobs. Regardless of the need, nothing can ever convince the men in the ranks that one of their number could not have filled jobs just as well. And generally speaking, they are right. Our men know that when vacancies occur they will be filled from their ranks. They are assured that advancement is controlled solely by their ability and the opportunities as they occur.

In addition to all these advantages, the board system produces another great asset, a willingness to seek and value the knowledge and opinions of others. This differs subtly but definitely from purely passive tolerance of other people's

ideas and opinions. New ideas are usually a synthesis or out-
growth of several concepts which we have gathered from
various sources. Our wisdom is the result of our own personal
experiences and the collective wisdom of the ages, passed
along to us through books, music, conversation, art, living
people, the drama, and a hundred other media. Even the
theories and inventions of men such as Einstein and Edison
are formulated this way; by further exploration of paths
already started, or by putting together several apparently
disconnected thought ingredients to produce a new idea. The
old adage "Two heads are better than one" can be expanded
endlessly if administrative techniques can be devised to avoid
mere idle speculation, opinionated thinking, and subsequent
confusion. By establishing a concept of group or team accomplishment, rather than individual competition, the board system encourages co-operative thinking and quells the natural
tendency to seek recognition and promotion through individual efforts. It is another tool in the emancipation of man from
"the tyranny of his own ego."

Therefore, the success of the entire system depends on the
maintenance of esprit de corps and individual morale and
good will. As no significant improvement is accomplished
singlehanded, the constructive attitude of everyone must be
maintained. Otherwise, the combination of individual abilities
is ineffective.

Here, then, is one of the real secrets of Multiple Management. For the board system not only throws together men of
diverse talents, but in operation it causes them to recognize
their interdependence. Again, this feeling, acquired in board
meetings, carries over into the entire managerial atmosphere.
Our supervisors are not practicing clever psychology when
they look to their people for help and suggestions. They have
come to realize that we can all learn something from each

other—and the man on the job is often the man best fitted to give advice about it. In such an atmosphere of security and mutual trust, our workers feel completely free to release the constructive talents inherent in them. How great that latent power can be, once released from brooding over management's unfairness, is one of the great revelations of the coming decade —the power of people.

CHAPTER V

THE JUNIOR BOARD

BEFORE the Junior Board began to function, I was a little afraid that in some instances the men would be carried away by their enthusiasm and would be inclined to try out highly risky ideas at the expense of the company. But in actual practice, this flaw never materialized. In fact, the general attitude of the board has been one of caution, especially where expense is an important factor.

The minutes of the first meetings showed that some fantastic projects had been suggested and tough battles had been fought over them, but under the rule that all recommendations must be unanimous, these proposals were modified in discussion or else turned down.

The recommendations that emerged proved, almost without exception, to be remarkably practical and economically sound. In its first five years the Junior Board made 2,109 unanimous suggestions to the Senior Board and of this number only six were rejected.

Even in the depression, the business made great strides. According to the records, much of the credit for this progress should go to the Junior Board.

One of the first problems it tackled was the repackaging of many of our items. Several of the young men embarked on a critical discussion of the traditional package of the extract business—a tall, thin, paneled bottle that was as old as the industry itself and was used by practically every extract manufacturer in the United States.

Some members of the Junior Board contended that this bottle had many faults, retarded sales, and should be changed. Opposed to them were a minority of the Junior Board and most of the Senior Board, who argued that the design of the old bottle, because of its long and widespread use, possessed important trade-mark value.

When the proposal to change the extract bottle reached a deadlock, the Junior Board, as a compromise, voted for a consumer research project, which was promptly approved by the Senior Board. Several thousand women were questioned as to their preferences and nearly all objected to our tall paneled bottles. They complained that these bottles slid out of hands slippery with shortening, toppled over too readily, and frequently fell from kitchen tables. Backed by these research findings, the Junior Board easily won its point about changing the bottle shape. A designer studied the results of the consumer investigation and then produced a much improved container. The change produced an immediate and substantial increase in flavoring extract sales.

Encouraged by this success, the Junior Board turned from extract bottles to the packaging of the entire line. None of the members liked the old-fashioned labels on many of the items and said so in plain language. So labels and packages were modernized and colors were harmonized, without any sacrifice of trade-mark value. In this redesigning, a prime consideration was that packages should have plenty of eye appeal on store counters.

The emphasis on eye appeal led to the proposal that the company install a model grocery store in its general offices, so that all packages could be studied from the consumers' angle and so retail dealers could be furnished with suggestions for store construction, interior planning, and effective displays. The model store was built and has proved a great asset, both for use in studying package displays and for retailers eager to renovate their stores at moderate cost. In discussions on the contents of the store, a lively dispute arose between the younger and older boards. The Junior Board wanted to display the goods of several competitors in the model store. This suggestion dismayed Senior Board members, who saw no reason for exhibiting and advertising the products of the opposition. In rebuttal, the Junior men argued that certain competitive products were standard in the trade, were found on the shelves of the best retailers, and that one of the best ways of demonstrating the superiority of our own goods would be to have them studied in contrast with the wares of other firms. The Junior Board won its point.

One of the most interesting of the board projects, one that has attracted comment all over the country, was the erection of an Old English tearoom and museum. In too many plants, the visiting salesman is treated like an unwelcome intruder— he waits for his appointment on a hard bench in a draughty anteroom. The Junior Board called a special meeting to explore a plan to erect an Old English tearoom, where salesmen, customers, and visitors could relax comfortably and enjoy a cup of tea while waiting to see company executives. The original proposal, as presented to the board, called for the creation of "an atmosphere of real hospitality" and suggested that this would be an excellent means of educating people to appreciate the deliciousness of properly brewed tea.

After some discussion, the chairman of the board requested each member to express his opinion. Although there was some adverse criticism of details, all members approved the basic idea. Despite this enthusiasm, the board displayed its customary caution and appointed a committee of three to determine costs and investigate other aspects of the scheme. When the committee had reported favorably and had come through with a specific plan, construction started on the tearoom.

Today on the seventh floor of our twentieth-century plant you can enter a simulated Elizabethan street, complete with stone house fronts, paneled doors, windows of leaded glass, and a stuffed pigeon squatting on a thatched roof. The Tea House roof is of thick, red, handmade tiles, the outside walls are of stone and timber. A sign by the lantern informs visitors that this is "Ye Olde McCormick Tea House." When guests step inside, they enter a room with a beamed ceiling and paneled walls, which is aglow from a fire in the massive grate. A girl in historic gown serves steaming cups of the choicest brews.

This building symbolizes the spirit of the company. We believe in friendliness in business and we think that the Tea House furnishes an encouraging atmosphere for the expression of such friendliness in buying and selling.

While the Tea House was being erected, the board approved a resolution to build a structure next door, to be used as a tea museum. The only one of its kind in the country, the museum has become an attractive addition to our promotional equipment. These structures have only indirect advertising value. However, they have attracted many hundreds of visitors to our display floor and we know their cost was a profitable investment. To me, these Elizabethan additions are a constant and pleasing reminder of the worth of young ideas in a modern business.

We had served tea to our employees at morning and afternoon rest periods for several years and had found that what had begun as a helpful gesture had paid off on the production charts. A rest period of 5 per cent of the working day resulted in a production increase of 9 per cent. No one thought of using this practice to help promote sales, until a Junior Board member revealed that we were the only large organization serving tea to its people. So a committee wrote a circular letter explaining the advantages of tea as a stimulant during the workday and in neighborly fashion offered the loan of thirty-cup tea pots. Within a few weeks several companies decided to try the plan and it developed into a successful sales project.

Naturally, not all of the Junior Board's ideas were so unusual. But through the years it has poked into almost every corner of the company's business, from the products themselves to their merchandising and advertising to foreign business to office procedures. Its suggestions have ranged from having airplanes drop circulars on open-air meetings to means of getting our tea served during the afternoon to all passengers on Baltimore and Ohio trains.

At one of the early meetings the board focused upon our line of products for household pets. We thought the line, which had been inaugurated about six years previous, was doing nicely, but the board thought otherwise. It outlined a special sales campaign, suggested trying it on a local level in Baltimore. So we arranged for retailers a special offer featuring dog remedies, soaps, insecticides, bird food, and the like. The offer not only procured a large number of window displays, but also boosted sales of pet products and the Junior Board recommended that the plan be adopted nationally.

Besides pushing old products, the Junior Board urged additions to our drug line and even instigated several valuable changes in formulae. Other suggestions for product improvement and expansion, as taken from the minutes, were:

Mr. ———— suggested that consideration be given to adding . . . to the line. He brought out the fact that one account alone, to his knowledge, uses over $30,000 worth of this material annually. Approved.

Dr. ——— (Chemist) mentioned that he had recently attended a citation hearing regarding the misbranding of Boric Acid, and while our present label was found to be in accord with regulations, it was his suggestion that we study all our labels to avoid the necessity of having officials bring them to our attention. Approved.

Mr. ——— suggested that consideration be given to an assortment including household insecticides and Red Arrow Garden Spray as the majority of hardware accounts now purchasing either of these items would probably be interested in both.

Mr. ——— also suggested that some plan be formulated to appeal to the junior gardener. This would include an educational leaflet ... and would be given only to those who purchased bottles of Red Arrow. Such a plan probably would have the endorsement of schools, all of which have classes in botany and biology.

After the board had been functioning six or seven months, it furnished us with another surprise. Just why it turned its attention to our Canadian business I do not know, but evidently one of the members thought we could increase our trade with the Dominion. At any rate, the board passed a resolution that an official of the company be sent to Canada for three months as a sort of good-will ambassador and outlined a plan for building up Canadian business. The purpose was not so much to write a lot of orders as to establish more cordial relations with distributors. The "ambassador" made the trip and the results were most gratifying.

Sometimes the board improved practices within the plant to save us money. For example, a member reported that the charge for outside telephone calls had increased steadily for several years and that he thought many of the calls were unnecessary. A letter was written to all employees. As a result, thanks to employee co-operation, the number of outside calls declined 50 per cent in a single month.

Another economy concerned the preservation of Ediphone and Dictaphone cylinders. We had found this system of dictation excellent except for the expense of replacing carelessly broken and damaged cylinders. The board spent some time with this problem, investigating and experimenting, and finally evolved a system which has worked well. Now each person who dictates is given a sufficient number of cylinders, bearing his initials, for which he is personally responsible. The Ediphone and Dictaphone department keeps a check on all cylinders. If the transcriber does not immediately report damaged cylinders as soon as he receives them, he is personally responsible. Within a week after this plan was put into effect, damage to cylinders decreased to a negligible amount.

Any innovation, no matter how enticing it may sound on the surface, has always been carefully scrutinized as to the expense involved. Looking over some old minutes, I found this paragraph:

Mr. ——— exhibited a layout of a Neon light sign for the roof of our building. Estimated cost about $4,000 a year. Each member present was asked for his individual criticism and practically everyone thought it too expensive, considering the results to be obtained. Not enough people would see the sign to justify the expense, it being more or less a local proposition. All felt that $4,000 annually could be spent to much better advantage either in selling or advertising. *Disapproved.*

No phase of the business has eluded the eyes of the Junior Board. It has discussed matters which are held sacrosanct to top management in most concerns, such as sales of common stock. For a number of years we have found that the sale of stock to our people was a wise policy because it trains them to save, ties them in with the affairs of the business, and creates greater interest in the company's general policies and its advancement. The board showed us a way to increase sales.

One Junior Board member recommended:

That the management give to those who have subscribed to a definite amount of stock on the partial payment plan, a paid-up stock certificate to the extent of the money already paid against their purchases. In other words, if a party had subscribed to ten shares of stock and he now has a little over half paid, he is entitled to a stock certificate for five shares and he may immediately resubscribe for ten shares.

Someone else suggested another method:

In order to increase the amount of shares sold, perhaps payments could be arranged for an extended period of four years at no additional cost over what is being paid by the buyers. This would enable the buyers to take on more stock.

Both plans won the favor of the Senior Board.

Other subjects at the board meetings were more mundane, but still important. Among the topics that have been discussed over the years are: the dead stock list, routing magazines through the office, discontinuance of slow sellers, changing the bylaws, sales follow-up on dormant accounts, familiarizing junior executives with manufacturing operations, a survey of correspondence, auditing cash sales and city order sheets, dispatching of merchandise, subscription to the trucking code, standard correspondence pads for salesmen, dental clinic prices, and dittoing export orders.

To show the conscientious and thorough manner in which the Junior Board has assumed its task, I have selected at random a few of its activities, as shown by the minutes:

Messrs. ———— and ———— appointed a committee to study the Order Department and make a report to the Junior Board.

Mr. ———— requested that all mail be signed and dispatched so that it can get out of the building earlier. He cited the case of Mr. ———— in New York who received his mail in the ten-o'clock delivery instead of an earlier delivery, because the mail was not received at the Baltimore Post Office until after six o'clock.

City Order Department: Mr. ———— reported that he could handle anywhere from 35 to 40 per cent more business with the same personnel. He asked for suggestions on ways to increase the city business.

Familiarizing junior executives with manufacturing operation: Dr. ——— suggested that the junior executives take more active interest in the manufacturing operation and that they assemble on a specified evening, to go in the manufacturing departments and, with the co-operation of the foremen, operate some of the lines of production, the junior executives doing the actual manual work. This was unanimously approved.

Use of stapling machines: Mr. ——— recommended that the use of stapling machines and staples in lieu of pins and clips be investigated. Messrs. ——— and ——— were appointed as a committee to look into the number of stapling machines required, together with the cost, and submit a report to the Junior Board.

Entertaining Baltimore retail grocers: Mr. ——— reported on the plan of entertaining the retail grocers of Baltimore and their wives and briefly outlined the plan of inviting the guests, beginning on April 5 and every Thursday thereafter, until all are invited. A trip through the building, movies and refreshments are to be included in the program. Approved.

Wholesale grocers' convention: Mr. ——— requested that the junior executives give consideration to the best novelty souvenirs to be given with the compliments of McCormick & Company at this convention, to be held in Chicago on June 18. Mechanical pencils were suggested and approved.

Suitable brief catalogue for jobbing salesmen: Mr. ——— recommended that a setup be made of four or five special loose-leaf sheets to fit the standard jobbing salesman's catalogue book to include all of the items in the line, with small cuts of the spice and tea cans, along with the extract bottle and mustard jar, to be compiled and sent out to jobbers and their salesmen upon request. Mr. ——— reported that he had conferred with Mr. ——— regarding this and thought that probably the Buyers' Guide could be reduced in size and perforated in order to answer the same purpose. Messrs. ——— and ——— were appointed a committee to work on this.

Mr. ——— reported that the new relish spread with a salad dressing base would be ready for distribution in a few days.

Mr. ——— mentioned the Relief Association dance to be held

on Friday, April 13, and asked for the co-operation of all junior executives.

Mr. ———— reported on the visit of the group of out-of-town retailers that will spend a Monday and Tuesday (date to be decided later) in May here at the plant, and requested the junior executives to sponsor this group and act as their hosts both in Washington and in Baltimore.

CHAPTER VI

THE FACTORY BOARD

DURING its first, experimental year, the Junior Board so quickly demonstrated its power for constructive action that we decided to establish a Factory Board. We called a meeting of all the factory foremen and department heads and assured them that, while the "front office" always would be willing to help, the organization was theirs, to be run under their management and without interference. To some people this looked like sheer foolhardiness. The Junior Board plan worked, they probably said to themselves, because its men were of potential executive caliber, while the Factory Board members were all men of little formal schooling and training who had come up from the ranks. Furthermore, once the workers were encouraged to speak their minds, they might bombard the board with gripes and a lot of dissension over labor policies might result.

The factory foremen and department heads decided on a membership of nine men, whom they named, and to this group added four observers, who would be probationary members and not hold actual office. It was agreed that the board would elect a chairman and secretary for a period of two months and, at the close of each period, advance the secretary to the chairmanship and elect his successor.

Once the organization was settled, the Factory Board tackled its assignment with startling speed.

At the first meeting, one member produced figures to show

40

that too many tea and spice cans were carried in stock. Remedial measures were taken and another problem, delays in receiving raw materials, was examined. Board members were determined to learn as much as they could about each and every section of the plant, as is shown by this excerpt from the minutes:

Due to various processes of manufacture, several departments are so closely intermingled that to study one without the other would be folly. As the drug department is at present being reorganized, it was decided to meet at 10 a.m. Wednesday in the laboratory, where the machinery used in supplying material to the drug department is to be inspected and its uses explained.

At the second session, in addition to the tour of inspection in the laboratory, members discussed general manufacturing methods—the introduction of better and less expensive production processes; improving the conveyor belts that delivered finished products to bottling and packaging machines; handling of three important products; preventing the leakage of stored materials; and the wisdom of installing a centralized stockroom for corrugated boxes and packers.

At the third meeting, the board appointed a committee of two to study the whole problem of corrugated boxes, ordered it to visit other industrial plants in the city using centralized stockrooms and to "obtain as much information as possible about their operation." The operations of the drug department were discussed, with suggestions made for more efficient handling of several products, for saving both effort and expense in the labeling processes, and for rearrangement of certain machines to effect economies. At the meeting, the board voted to request a monthly supper meeting in addition to the regular weekly meetings.

Occasionally, the Factory Board suggested steps which would have been taken with poor grace by the workers if they

had come from top management. For example, during its first
year the board made some recommendations about work
clothes—coats should be provided for mechanics and possibly
for the guides, while all workmen should wear neat, attractive
clothes of a uniform nature. As a rule, factory workers hate
wearing uniforms and, if these recommendations had been
handed down as orders from above, I think there would have
been resentment. The motions were carried forward for several meetings, then finally passed and put into effect. There
were no objections whatever from employees and I think that,
in most cases, they rejoiced because they no longer had to
worry about "work clothes."

Ever since the company had established the time-clock system many years ago, we had been annoyed by substitute
punching. We had adopted rules and issued orders, but all to
no avail, until the factory executives unanimously passed this
resolution:

Anyone punching a number on a time-clock other than his own
should be immediately dismissed from our service.

Again the Factory Board demonstrated that its decrees carried
much more force than the old management's. Today we have
no time clocks at all and no apparent need for them.

Factory cleanliness was always another touchy problem
until the board became interested in it. The subject arose again
and again and finally the board recommended:

That a committee be appointed to inspect the plant weekly and
that the awards in the form of stars on the bulletin boards—a blue
star for poor housekeeping, a silver star for fair housekeeping and
a gold star for good housekeeping. The awards are to be made
monthly.

Although the plan was adopted unanimously, it did not
work too well, since personal opinion frequently entered into

the appraisals. Undaunted, the board decided to try a rating chart. Each department was graded under such general headings as floors and aisles, machinery and equipment, stock, employees, and safety; and such subheadings as condition of walls, tidiness of uniforms, arrangement and care of stock, and the hands and hair of workers. The results of this more objective rating can be seen in our spotless plant and spick-and-span personnel.

Among the several hundred subjects considered by the Factory Board in its first year were rearrangement of storage rooms, machinery and routine, checks on blunders made outside the factory which hurt production, standardization of packages, placing of improved machinery, uniformity of the quality of products, elimination of dust and other fire hazards, reduction of trucking costs, prompt disposal of complaints, and a factory library.

At one time, the Factory Board sent a request to the Junior Board to see that all details of new packages and goods were worked out completely before samples were sent to salesmen and the items placed in production. The result was not only a fine display of teamwork, but the elimination of expense and annoyance. Many times in the past, in our anxiety to start selling new products, we had burdened the factory with orders for goods that were not ready for shipment, but I do not think this will ever happen again.

Another farsighted move of the Factory Board was the establishment of a school for foremen and assistants. The board also broadened its scope to include civic affairs and requested all factory executives to recommend young men and women who might be trained to assist in the annual Community Fund drive.

Reviewing the minutes of the Factory Board during its first year, I noted that the new management had established itself more quickly and efficiently than we had anticipated. The board spent little time on workers' gripes. Labor relations were the least of its troubles and never had factory routine run so smoothly. In fact, it was surprising to note how many men, who had been known for radical tendencies, became ultraconservative after studying the activities of our entire organization for a few months. It is not unusual for a Factory Board member to declare that our workers are being petted and pampered and it is sometimes necessary to prevent the board from leaning over backwards in the administration of discipline. Once, when I dropped in at a meeting, I found the members about to fire two workers who had broken rules. Jobs were scarce then and I had to plead the case of the men for some time to convince the board that they deserved another chance.

Naturally, the accomplishments of the Factory Board in improving methods, slicing costs, and increasing profits were invaluable to the company. But of greater worth, in my opinion, was the attitude that board members assumed unconsciously after the first few meetings. They began to show that poise and thoughtfulness which distinguishes all men when they realize their responsibility to their fellows and share the obligations of the success of a business. The men in the factory had learned that there were no cinch jobs in the company, that the front office personnel worked tirelessly, and that the salesmen performed a difficult task, essential to the welfare of all. At the end of the year every man in the organization showed more respect for the other fellow's contribution.

In my opinion, this was the most important year in the company's long history, because during that time we proved that the principles of multiple business control could be applied to the factory as well as the office management of the organization. And in the proving not only our factory executives, but the members of our Junior and Senior Boards, as well as practically all of our employees, had come to a broader understanding of the new management.

Although the Factory Board easily demonstrated its merits within the plant, on the outside some strange rumors circulated in the trade and among other manufacturers. They gossiped that we were allowing our employees to run our business completely. And nothing could have been further from the truth. Throughout our development of Multiple Management, we impressed upon all board members that their decisions needed the approval of the higher authorities, either the president or the Senior Board of Directors. From the start, our workers understood that we were not changing the form of our management, but improving it and extending it to all departments of the business.

During the second and subsequent years, the Factory Board naturally functioned much more smoothly. It spent a good deal of time amending the bylaws, so they could stand for several years to come and, because members had learned more about parliamentary procedure, the meetings were run more efficiently and the elections held with a minimum of discussion. The members had studied all the manufacturing processes and had learned something about selling and advertising. Many mysteries had been cleared up. The first action taken at the outset of the second year was the adoption of a pledge, signed by all members, which placed each member on record as affirming the purpose and spirit of the factory organization.

While all the activities of the Factory Board would be far too numerous to mention, here are some projects of special interest, which will show the scope of its investigations:

Visits to the factory. The board always welcomed tours through the factory of both the trade and consumers. On one occasion, a good customer, a big wholesale grocery concern, could make the trip only on a Saturday morning. Because the Factory Board wanted to show the plant as a going concern, it passed a resolution that the employees work a half day on Friday and a half day on Saturday. With this went a request that "everyone be on his mettle during the inspection and that we have as much machinery working as possible." Thanks to the spirit displayed, the visit was a marked success.

Fights between workers. These had occurred only infrequently and the usual practice had been a brief investigation by foremen and the personnel director, which was followed by firing of the instigator. In the third year of the board's tenure, when a fight disrupted routine, the factory executives determined to conduct a thorough investigation to see that justice was done. After a careful search for the facts, the board learned that one man had criticized a second, which led to an exchange of curses, then an attack with a wooden stick by one of the participants, who was prepared to capitalize on his gains with a hatchet. The board gave both men opportunity to appear before it and fully state their cases, for which they both expressed thanks. One was retained in the company, the other permitted to resign.

Waste disposal. Through the action of a special committee, a great deal of oil was recovered and sold, and higher prices obtained for old machinery, spice and flour bags, barrels, junk iron, and other materials.

Minimum wages. A survey by several board members showed that McCormick was paying more than the prevailing wage rate in Baltimore. The board endorsed this policy, claiming that higher wages would attract more efficient workers.

Old employees. One of our most serious problems was what to do about the employees who had grown old in the service of the company and who did not want to be pensioned off. A recommendation was made and adopted that all the older workers, including those approaching pension age and those who wanted to stay on after 65, should be given handwork exclusively. Several processes which could not be handled by machines—the weighing and packing of stick cinnamon, the handling of special orders, and other jobs—were concentrated in one department and the work turned over to the older workers, who could proceed at a leisurely pace at tasks where dimming eyesight and hearing make little difference. Several of these older workers have told me how wonderful it is to be independent at their age and to know they are still useful.

A suggestion was made to install a mechanical handling system for mayonnaise and extract bottles. After a thorough discussion a motion was unanimously approved that this suggestion be accepted as it will materially cut down the cost of handling and storing bottles.

A suggestion was made to store alcohol and vinegar in tanks. A motion was unanimously approved that alcohol and vinegar be stored in tanks so as to purchase these two items in tank-car lots instead of drum lots. This would cut down the cost per gallon plus handling and the saving would enable us to pay for these tanks within fifteen months.

A suggestion was made to purchase additional extract percolators. After a thorough discussion it was brought out that we could produce additional extract with the same operators. A motion was unanimously approved that these additional percolators be purchased.

A suggestion was made that we purchase an automatic packer for our food colors at a cost of approximately $15,000. After careful consideration it was decided that a saving could be realized from this packer and it would pay for itself within three years. A motion was unanimously approved that we purchase same.

A suggestion was made to install ultra violet ray lamps and glyco spray units in various departments to prevent colds, which would help to cut down absenteeism during the winter months. A motion was unanimously approved that it be accepted.

Sooner or later, all organizations inevitably fall into a rut. This happened to the Factory Board, which at one time bogged down in old business or new business of little moment. The next day, in reading the minutes, I detected a tendency to magnify the unimportant, to pay undue respect to personality, and to devote too much time to nonessentials. So I wrote the board that this tendency, if not checked, would reduce its activities to mere window dressing. The board made some attempt at defending itself, but did admit that it had slipped into a groove. Once the problem was faced it faded and the board dug in with new vigor.

Many companies tend to become so involved in their own affairs that they ignore everything about the competition except sales figures. But the Factory Board has always shown a keen interest in other spice concerns, and in the methods of other businesses generally, and has learned when to profit from others' experiences and when to be proud of McCormick superiority. Once a member of the Junior Board, after a trip to several competitors and distributors, reported that our manufacturing methods were in some ways inferior to those of other companies and that one distributor had criticized the packing of certain products. The factory executives immediately tried to rectify these faults. At another time a committee of the Factory Board visited a large plant near Baltimore, where the goods manufactured were totally unrelated to spices, and brought back a better method of keeping a running inventory, plus other valuable ideas. The board has always encouraged visits to other companies and we have always swapped ideas freely, learning much from others in return.

Some time after this incident I wrote a letter to a trade association deploring the spiritless submission to cheap competition on the part of many spice firms and offering several remedies for this. The letter came up for discussion at a Factory Board meeting. One member compared one of our products, which cost $1.14 a dozen to make, with a product made by a small manufacturer working in an "unclean cellar" with the "very cheapest materials," which cost only 72 cents a dozen. He concluded: "While it is true that our goods are superior and that we constantly urge our salesmen to sell on highest quality, but not on price, it is also necessary for us to try to reduce our manufacturing expenses by increased efficiency, to meet this competition." To have discussions of this type among our factory executives, with the accumulation of knowledge they indicate, was worth all the time and trouble required to establish the Factory Board. Such interest and understanding have helped us to lower factory costs and to increase wages, volume, and profits.

CHAPTER VII

THE SALES BOARD—SPARKPLUG OF MANAGEMENT

ALTHOUGH the last of the four major boards organized, the Sales Board is second to none in importance. As competition increased and the battle for markets grew tighter, the Sales Board assumed even greater responsibilities. We could produce all we could sell—but we could not sell all we produced. And the deeper the Junior and Factory Boards delved into the business the more they turned to sales problems. At the same time they saw the need for constant advice and consultation from the advertising and sales departments.

Nor was this the only reason for setting up a Sales Board. In any company the salesman's job is a tough one. In too many companies it is also a thankless one. Out on the road alone, under the pressure of all kinds of competition selling, with the sales manager and his quota pressing on his back, it is not strange that the salesman often feels like a distant relative. On his infrequent trips to the home office he sees an apparently well-integrated group of people going about established daily tasks, and he contrasts this feeling of security and "feeling at home" with his own life on the road. (He may not contrast his salary with these others, although he would be happier if he did.) At any rate, he often gets the feeling that he's on the outside, looking in. And along with that he may think that top management really doesn't know as much about his problems as it does about the problems of the factory and office personnel. The net result is a decrease in the salesman's efficiency, a decline in sales, and increased distribution costs. One aspect of this discontent is the current trend toward unionization among sales forces, even where the men earn high salaries. It's the old story. If management doesn't look out for the welfare of its workers, they organize and fight for their rights as a group. This happened with foremen, and it now is happening with salesmen.

The McCormick Sales Board presented a slightly different organizational problem from other boards. We wanted to have the salesmen well represented, but in the beginning we felt it necessary to include a certain number of home office executives, in order to give the board some direction. Moreover, we wanted to throw the salesmen members into close contact with men on the planning and administrative side in order to educate both groups.

Top membership of the board is presently set at twenty active members, consisting of fifteen outside sales representatives and five associate nonvoting members, all chosen from the outside sales organization. As always, members cannot hold office on other boards, and a rotation system is provided. Board membership carries the usual directors' fees and extra profit-sharing bonuses. Men with the best sales records are naturally favored for board posts, but other consideration enters into elections.

Because board members are scattered from coast to coast, the semimonthly meetings held by the Factory and Junior Boards are impractical. Instead, the Sales Board meets twice a year for a week-long session. Between these semiannual meetings, board business is carried on by committees, operating around a home office nucleus and co-ordinated by mail and phone.

Complete reports on all board developments and committee

meetings are sent to each salesman, who is thus kept up to the minute on all important aspects of merchandising, advertising, and distributing policies. At the same time, the men in the field are encouraged to write frankly, offering either suggestion or complaint, as the case may be. The semiannual meetings provide plenty of opportunity for fun and relaxation, as well as working sessions. Salesmen are less shy about speaking their minds than other workers, and the lid is really off whenever our men meet. But the net result to date has always been greater efficiency and teamwork.

Just as the Junior and Factory Board members found their interests were linked to sales problems, so did the Sales Board find the answers to some of its headaches could be got only by questioning purchasing, storage, office management, shipping, and other procedures. Sales Board members found improvements in some of these areas, and in getting the answers to them they began to realize some of the problems faced by the office and factory people. And once again, understanding led to better teamwork.

Including the advertising department's representatives in the Sales Board program was another move that pulled our sales and distribution machinery into a smooth-working machine. Today it is fairly common to find market research, sales promotion, merchandising, and sales working as an integral unit, but fifteen years ago, when we first made this move, it was unusual. Even today, some companies still keep their advertising departments out on a limb, working away from the main body of sales effort.

Our semiannual meetings follow certain broad agenda, but the program is never so fixed that it cannot be interrupted for an immediate discussion of new ideas developed at the meeting. We usually start the ball rolling with a complete report on the company's status, including profit statements, sales·

volume, and new policy changes in any department for the coming half year. Then, after a discussion of this and other matters on the managerial agenda, the salesmen members go to bat, bringing up the various suggestions, complaints, and problems brought to their attention by our sales force. Naturally, only top policy questions are debated at this meeting; the minor headaches are handled via the usual board committee machinery.

Here, for example, is a typical recent Sales Board recommendation, which was studied by a committee, adopted by the Sales Board in a regular meeting, and then approved by management and put into effect. It set up a new sales training program for the company which has proved successful.

The following is a general outline for sales training designed to be applicable to any region within the sales territory of McCormick & Company:

1. It will be the responsibility and duty of each regional director to see that each executive salesman within the region is properly instructed in the mechanics of training thoroughly, a new sales employee coming into the region.

2. The regional director will administer the "Training The Trainer" program, details of which are given in full below, within his region. This program will take the form of a series of classes to be conducted by the regional director. The instruction pattern to be followed is prescribed in Part 1 of "Training The Trainer."

3. The regional director will administer the "Training The Trainee" program which is to be followed by the trainer who will indoctrinate the new sales employee. (See Part 2 of the Sales Training Outline.) This schedule is to run for a two-week period. At the conclusion of the two-week course, the regional director will give the trainee a check out which will serve as a final examination prior to the assignment of the trainee to a territory.

4. It is recommended that management give thought and consideration to the idea of a text to be used as a supplement to the sales training guide. It is suggested that this text incorporate all

details outlined in Section I of the Sales Training Outline—"Training The Trainer."

SALES TRAINING OUTLINE

PART 1—"TRAINING THE TRAINER"

I. All facts pertaining to the Organization of McCormick and Company.
  A. *Human Relations.* To include thorough review of Profit Sharing Trust, Pension Plan, Company Insurance (Beneficial Association, Group Life and Hospitalization, Auto Insurance, etc.), Vacations, Incentives, Future and Security.
  B. History of the Business.
  C. Current trends within McCormick and Company.
  D. Multiple Management, its inception, true meaning, structure and functions of various boards, etc.

II. All facts pertaining to functional Sales practice.
  A. Baltimore Plan—Program selling, Ten points, supplementary points of Who buys—what, where, when, how much, what makes a merchant buy.
  B. Instruction in practical application of Baltimore Plan to all types of trade to include retail, jobbing, chain accounts.
  C. Selling mechanics—through jobber, direct, drop shipments, warehouse.
  D. Tools of the trade, proper use thereof. To include catalogues, Brochure, Sample Cases, Merchandising Kits, Products Digest, Inventory control book, Route Cards, Sales Training Manual, Tea Hex, etc.
  E. Forms to be used—H-170, H-191, Order forms, etc.
  F. General Conduct on the trade. He, as a representative of McCormick and Company—poise, know how.

PART 2—"TRAINING OF THE NEW SALES EMPLOYEE"

I. Schedule to be followed for two weeks.
  A. *Indoctrination*—First day of first and second weeks. Breaking this up from a straight two days will eliminate confusion in the mind of the new employee, and allow him to assimilate better the basic information given him. This

indoctrination will include all points as incorporated in Paragraphs I and II of Part 1.

B. *Retail Training*—Two days, plus or minus, will be consumed with trainer and trainee on ·retail trade. Repeat 2nd week.

C. *General Training*—Balance of week, two days, plus or minus, to be spent covering normal duties with the Executive Salesman which include jobber and/or chain accounts. Repeat 2nd week.

D. *Instruction Training in the line*—Insofar as possible a new sales employee will be trained at either the Executive or Regional headquarters. His point, at discretion of Regional Director.

Conclusion

The program as outlined above is offered as a guide and possible solution for the reinstatement of the "Mc" college idea for the training of sales personnel in each Region within the sales organization of this firm.

Supplementary Suggestions or Amendments

1. It is further recommended that the "Training The Trainer" program be accomplished in all regions by November 1, 1947.

2. Employment of new men will be a joint responsibility of the Regional Director and Executive Salesman.

The work of the board is particularly valuable in organizing our annual sales convention. It relieves the executive head of much labor and from doing more than an adequate share of the talking. It furnishes new speakers, many unusual subjects of value, and it has proved itself to be an inspiring factor in promoting and managing the conventions.

The performance of our Sales Board, over the years, has established it as a permanent fixture. Its recommendations have been worth many times the expense entailed in setting up and operating the board, and its indirect values are inestimable. All our salesmen know that new ideas or plans for the improvement of sales, or anything else in their field that they submit to the board, will be seriously discussed and evaluated by their own kind—by men who are sales minded, who speak the salesman's language.

Many of our salesmen, as well as other members of our organization, own common stock in the company. We have found, almost invariably, that the most aggressive and successful salesmen are the ones who are the heaviest owners of stock. As with all other classes of employees, stock ownership ties the salesman in with the affairs of the business, trains him to save, and creates a greater interest in the general policies and advancement of the company.

Initially, in organizing the Sales Board, we thought it necessary to include as members five home office executives of experience and conservative judgment. We thought that a board composed entirely of salesmen, or even one on which the salesmen were in the majority, would not be so effective and might result in serious confusion. Actually, we changed this thinking when the Sales Board failed to ring the bell as quickly as the other boards. Now, composed entirely of salesmen, the Sales Board is one of our brightest success stories.

The Sales Board, like all the others, gives management an opportunity to find material for executive sales management. Its membership is composed of twenty of our most able salesmen. Under Multiple Management these men are given an insight into the complete management of the business and are instructed in the correlation of all divisions of the company. They are given every encouragement to broaden the application of their special talents and make their thinking more practical, and they understand that they are candidates for future positions as executives.

Our experience shows that after a Sales Board has had a little experience, it tackles market and technical analyses with surprising results. There is always a reason for the slumping of a territory or for a volume of business from a city or district that is not so large as it should be. Usually, the salesmen involved are blamed for conditions of this kind. Seldom is this blame justified, and it is gratifying to see our men go after the solution of sales problems after the facts have been presented.

Moreover, management can learn plenty from its sales force on the task of selling ideas and policies to the people. But as Mr. Robert Creaghead pointed out in a speech before the Association of National Advertisers, to do so properly may require some revised thinking. Said Mr. Creaghead:

Each function in industrial marketing has its counterpart in internal merchandising. Let's take a look at the principal ones, which are as follows:

Merchandising	Internal Merchandising
Market Research	Employee attitude and opinion studies
Sales policy	Organization policy
Product design	Organization structure
Distribution	Supervision
Catalogue	Foreman's Manual
Magazine advertising	Employee publication
Customer booklet	Employee manual
Direct mail	Letters to employees
Bill Board	Poster and bulletin boards
Radio	Public address system
Dealer training	Foreman training
Advertising Manager	Industrial Relations Director
Advertising Agent	Internal Public Relations Counselor

Basic Approach and Fundamentals   Both of these programs depend upon these fundamental premises:

1. Respect for citizens' right of choice
2. Understanding of his needs and wants
3. Consideration for his habits and modes of thought

But neither of these types of selling will succeed
without:

1. A well thought-out plan
2. Carried out as a long-range program
3. Composed of sound and believable material
4. Well presented, and
5. Maintained with continuity.

Just as you know that certain results can be expected in the market
by following certain programs, so you can be sure that selling ideas
to your employees can be planned and its results predicted with equal
confidence.

It is pointless to burden the reader further with a discussion
of our complete sales program. We place strong emphasis on
team quotas established on a realistic, attainable basis. Combined with sales bonuses on both an individual and a team
basis, and backed by a strong advertising campaign, promotion and merchandising tools and an expert market research
staff, we have increased our sales more than fivefold in the
past fifteen years. As with our complete human relations program, our sales administration is based on security, opportunity, and understanding. It pays off—for everyone, including the consumer, who enjoys lowered prices as the sales
volume moves upward steadily.

There is one other tool we use in developing a hard-hitting
sales force. It is axiomatic that success in the sales field is
more dependent on personality and character than success in,
let us say, machine-tool operation. Recognizing this, and seek-
ing again a scientific appraisal of our human problems, we
have called in a psychologist to evaluate the personality structure of our salesmen. We use this measurement, along with
a battery of other tests, to balance our own subjective judgments as to the merits and potentialities of the men. This fits
in again with our constant attempts toward correct job placement. In several instances we have been able to discover men

of unusual ability who were being stymied by some small quirk of a correctable nature. When approached in the right manner and handled tactfully, we have found such consultation as helpful and necessary among our more intellectual members, as normal medical care has proved for the rank-and-file worker.

Speaking of psychologists, I am reminded of the report made by one several years ago. Certain business friends of mine were skeptical about some of the gains we had made under Multiple Management. They had been told that when wages were increased 10 per cent in its first year, sales increased 10 per cent. And after the first three years, when we raised wages 42 per cent, our production stepped up 42 per cent. When we knocked off 5 per cent of our daily production time to give all our people a morning and afternoon cup of tea, the factory repaid this trust by producing 9 per cent more. The more they heard, the less they believed, and they finally ended up by asking me if I'd be willing to let a consulting psychologist come in and see what we had at McCormick & Company. Naturally, I agreed. And here's what the doctor reported, comparing McCormick employee attitudes to others:

Friendliness	versus	Aloofness
Energy	versus	Dissipation
Cooperation	versus	Conflict
Upgrading	versus	Importation
Understanding	versus	Directives
Confidence	versus	Fear
Merit	versus	Favoritism
Men	versus	Products
Results	versus	Motion
Leadership	versus	Force
Colleagues	versus	Bosses
Welfare	versus	Salesmanship
Integrity	versus	Intrigue
Helpfulness	versus	Criticism

All of which we were glad to learn. We knew we had something, but we had never ticked it off systematically. But now, to summarize on the Sales Board:

In our experience, a Sales Board is an essential part of Multiple Management. In many of the manufacturing organizations, I have studied, selling is considered as a factor apart from all other necessary activities, something more or less mysterious which requires special talents for its understanding. Frequently, in otherwise well-managed companies, selling is placed under one-man management. We have proved that sales problems can be grasped and corrected by any fairly intelligent individual, and that general understanding of sales problems throughout an organization smooths out many difficulties.

The knowledge of human relations and the power of people can best be researched in the above methods—through understanding of the other fellow's problem—and through service to others we learn how to please our customers best. That's the salesman's payoff—satisfied customers.

CHAPTER VIII

JUNIOR EXECUTIVES TAKE STOCK OF THEIR WORK

A CONTEST some years ago for the best letter on the advantages of being a Junior Executive Board member at McCormick & Company gave me an enlightened understanding of the attitudes of members toward their work. The winning letter was written by a young man who, within four years, worked himself up from a minor position to one of trust and responsibility. He is a charter member of the Junior Board, and I think his letter, which is representative of the ideas expressed by his colleagues, is well worth reading by everyone who is interested in Multiple Management. Here it is:

"To my mind, the greatest advantage presented to an ambitious young man by the Junior Board of Executives System is that it gives every young man in the business an opportunity to express his opinion on matters not of secondary nature, but the very problems that are of vital interest to the welfare of the company. This enables us to deviate distinctly from the old story of the conductor on the electric railroad who through his endless conversation tries to give the unfortunate bystander the impression that he knows more about running the railroad than the officers. Here, if you show just a glimmer of promise, you are elected to an organization or board which enables you to put forth your ideas, some of which may have real significance, and if approved by your fellow members are passed on for final approval by the directors. Now, if these ideas, resolutions, or whatever name they may be called, were merely tabled by the Senior Board and never heard from again, then the Junior Board for me would lack a great deal of its desirability. However, experience shows that almost all the recommendations made by the Junior Board to the Senior Board have been accepted, which does give a fellow a certain feeling of satisfaction that something really worthwhile is being accomplished and that he is something more than a glorified office boy or clerk waiting for his superior to die so that he may step into his place.

"Another thing, the Junior Board helps in more than one way to better prepare you to fill eventually your superior's position and at the same time have a better insight in the business which enables you not only to fill that immediate job but others. Through this channel you receive valuable information regarding the so-called inner facts of the organization that would take years to get otherwise. Because of this added knowledge, you take a greater interest in the business and try to grasp more threads which will help you to become of greater service. By the same token, the older men, realizing that you are striving to go ahead, take an even greater interest in you and materially help you on your way. This is demonstrated very distinctly by the interest our Senior Board members have shown in attending the meetings of the Junior Board where they have taken an active part and have brought many facts to the attention of this young and, as is the usual case with any board so comprised, more or less radically opinioned group. Sometimes we may lack the soberness of mature judgment, but that in turn may be good to help enliven the older group by seeing the reactions of younger men.

"Say what you will, the Junior Board gives a young man a certain feeling of self-confidence and, at times, a little self-satisfaction at having accomplished something. I realize that self-satisfaction in anything is bad, but in small doses it really does wonders for a fellow to think that in such a large organization as ours he has done some small service not actually required of him in his daily work. This to my way of thinking is the spark that makes a person strive for even greater things which eventually, if not now, will be the lifeblood of the Company.

"There is always the competitive spirit associated with the Junior Board which makes it interesting. You constantly realize that there are other people striving for your place and it is up to you to so produce as to stay there.

"The Junior Board has so many other features that to give them would require so much space and probably would become so boring that I prefer to sum them all up in one word, 'spirit.' I have never worked for any other company, but judging from the conversation of some of my friends who work elsewhere, I can readily see that our Junior Board gives its members a certain enthusiasm and desire of cooperation that is lacking elsewhere. This is the 'spirit' to which I refer and sincerely feel that the major portion of the success of any business is due to the cooperativeness of the people therein.

"The Junior Board is a step towards greater things and those that make the most creditable showing are the first to make additional strides."

Among the many other companies which have adopted Multiple Management, the Williamson Heater Company of Cincinnati has had one of the longest and most successful experiences. Recently, the executives of the Williamson Company (manufacturers of furnaces) asked me to come to Cincinnati to address a banquet commemorating the tenth anniversary of Multiple Management in their organization. What I said seemed to me less important than the things I heard from four men who had risen through Multiple Management to positions of responsibility in the Williamson organization.

I am reproducing here their remarks along with a brief

biographical sketch of each one. Their views are typical reactions of young men who have caught the spirit of Multiple Management:

<h3 style="text-align:center">J. P. ("BUCK") FIELD</h3>

Rank-and-File Capacities

Stock Boy—Sheet Metal	May, 1934-August, 1934
Order Picker—Sheet Metal Fittings	August, 1934-December, 1934
Press and Shear Operator	January, 1935-June, 1935
Assembler Sheet Metal Fittings	June, 1935-December, 1935

Management Capacities

Assistant Foreman Castings Shipping	January, 1936-December, 1936
Foreman—Fittings Shipping	January, 1937-December, 1937
Supervisor—Fittings Production Control	January, 1938-December, 1938
Foreman—Fittings Manufacturing	January, 1939-February, 1940
General Superintendent—Fittings Manufacturing	February, 1940-June, 1942
Fabricating Superintendent Armor Plate Division	June, 1942-December, 1942
Manufacturing Superintendent Aircraft Division	January, 1943-March, 1944
General Superintendent—all steel fabrication	March, 1944-September, 1945
Resident Manager—Madison, Indiana Plant	September, 1945-March, 1947
Factory Manager—Cincinnati Plant	April, 1947-March, 1948
Sales Manager—Sheet Metal Products	April, 1948 to present

Board Service

Elected to Factory Board—1939—still serving without interruption

TRUSTEE—The Williamson Heater Company Employees' Trust—December, 1941—still serving

Present Age . . . 39

Before we get into the subject at hand, I'd like to ask you a question—what are the factors that determine teamwork? Whether it be football, baseball, basketball or, yes, management teamwork, the answer is the same.

My first reaction, and I daresay yours, would be (using football as an example) the athletic director, the coaches, and the players; in short, people.

In my humble opinion there is little question on that point, but if we want to discuss good teamwork, there are a lot of factors that must be considered. There are the rules of the game to be considered, rules which the players as well as the coaches and athletic director must understand. There are the signals which must be understood. The player must know not only how to play his position, but must know the relation of his position to other positions. He must understand and be willing to do the things that will aid his teammates. He must understand and be willing to do the things that will aid the team as a whole. Many times, when we sit in the stands and watch one of our favorites make a broken-field run, we are so occupied with our thoughts of the outcome of his run that we fail to recognize the teamwork that made this oustanding run possible.

And so it is with our management team. On many occasions we center our attention on the broken field run and overlook the many elements that tend to build that all-important factor of teamwork.

Let me present this thought in another manner. Sometime when you have a spare moment close one eye and place a half dollar very close to and directly in front of the other eye. What do you see? All you can see is the half dollar. Now hold it at arm's length. What do you see? You see the half dollar, but you also see the people and you see other objects that together make the picture complete. Everything within the room now takes its rightful place. And so it must be with a team-spirited management.

Which brings me to the subject at hand: *What Has Multiple Management Meant to Me?*

Participation in Multiple Management has enabled me to gain a greater knowledge of the over-all operation of our Company. It has given me a greater appreciation of our Company policies and of why it is necessary for management to do certain things in certain ways, speaking as an individual who has, with my fellow supervisors, initiated actions that later became policy and later yet came down through line organization for execution: I feel a personal responsibility for seeing that these policies succeed. I feel a personal responsibility for seeing that they are thoroughly explained to every individual who looks to me for leadership, and in a manner which will create understanding.

Participation in Multiple Management has enabled me to better put my thoughts into writing. It has given me a confidence and improved my ability to stand on my feet and put my thoughts into words.

Participation in Multiple Management has permitted me to gain a better understanding of my fellow men. I have had the opportunity to observe each and every one of my fellow supervisors in action. I am familiar with how each supervisor reacts to certain approaches and how he thinks on certain subjects. Knowing these things I am in a better position to work in harmony with them, and they, knowing these things about me, are in a better position to work in harmony with me.

Through participation in Multiple Management I have learned a greater respect for the older men and their varied experiences, and how they apply these experiences when approaching problems. I have also learned a greater respect for the younger men with their abundant energy, their initiative, and their drive, and I have lived with and seen the accomplishments that can be attained by combining the two as a team.

Participation in Multiple Management has given me the feeling of being a very definite part of something. I don't feel left out. I feel that my contributions are recognized and appreciated. I feel that I am a definite part of the management team.

Participation in Multiple Management has built within me that sense of partnership which I believe causes an individual to contribute not only because he feels it best, but because he derives a certain sense of satisfaction through that contribution. It has built within me a desire to know more about my job, more about my company, and more about our system of free enterprise. It has built within me a desire to know more about people, more about their likes, their dislikes, more about their peculiarities, more about their reaction to certain conditions and changes, and why they react as they do.

I would like very briefly to contrast the feelings I have just expressed to those which I experienced before participating in Multiple Management. When I was promoted to a foreman position, I knew very little about our Company other than the department I was to supervise, and speaking very frankly I didn't care to learn too much about the Company other than the knowledge I needed to supervise the department I had been assigned. When I approached a problem it was in the light of how my department and the people in it would be affected. When I considered taking action on a subject, I did not consider how it would affect other departments or the Company as a whole. I felt that I could run my department and that it was up to the other supervisors to run their respective departments. I did not offer assistance to other supervisors and I resented any helpful suggestions that were offered with respect to my department.

Need I say more about what Multiple Management has done for me?

J. P. Field

G. W. DENGES

Rank-and-File Capacities

Blueprint Boy	June, 1926-March, 1927
Tracer	April, 1927-August, 1928
Draftsman	September, 1928-December, 1934

Management Capacities

Supervisor Application Engineering Department	January, 1935-January, 1936
Forced Air Sales and Service Engineer	February, 1936-January, 1937
Manager Air Conditioning and Blower Division	January, 1937-December, 1940
Sales and Engineering Representative — Government Defense Housing Projects	January, 1941-May, 1942
Chief Inspector—Aircraft and Armor Plate Divisions	May, 1942-December, 1942
Manager—Aircraft Division	January, 1943-August, 1945
Manager—Industrial Relations	August, 1945-December, 1946
Manager Product Development and Company representative on construction of Indiana Plants	January, 1947-January, 1948
General Sales Manager	February, 1948 to present

Board Service

Elected to Junior Board December, 1938—served until December, 1946

Elected to Factory Board December, 1946—served until December, 1947

Elected to Senior Board December, 1947—still serving

Elected Vice-President April, 1946—still serving

TRUSTEE—The Williamson Heater Company Employees' Trust—April, 1944—still serving

Present age . . . 38

The subject "What Multiple Management Has Meant to Me" offers an excellent opportunity to present a case history of just what has happened to me since the inception of Multiple Management ten years ago. To do this, however, in my opinion would only reveal the results of Multiple Management, with which we are all familiar, whereas I believe the causes of these results are of far greater importance.

There are many benefits which I feel I have derived from Multiple Management, such as a broader knowledge of our own business and a better understanding of business problems in general. This knowledge makes it possible for me to view current problems not only as they might affect my own department, but also the effect on the business as a whole. In addition, this knowledge makes it possible for me to meet new friends and be in a position to discuss current business problems with some degree of confidence.

Multiple Management has also provided the opportunity to offer suggestions and express my views on policies and operations of the business. This opportunity requires me to give suggestions and ideas careful thought and consideration, as I know they are subjected to questioning and criticisms of many others. This promotes *thinking* and in addition gives me a feeling of self-satisfaction in being able to *say* what I *think*.

There are many other benefits which I attribute to my experience in participating in Multiple Management, but the one which I feel has meant the most to me is the training I have received in working with others and seeing just what can be accomplished by working together as a team, rather than as individuals. This training has given me a better understanding of people and a respect for their desires and feelings, not only in matter of business, but personal as well. It has taught me to be cautious in my judgment of others and offer constructive criticism only when I am convinced it is needed. It has taught me to seek the advice and opinions of others, as I have learned that there is a tremendous store of knowledge at our disposal if we will only use it. It has taught me to share whatever knowledge I have been able to acquire with others, as in so doing I know the team will be stronger. It has given me the spirit of teamwork and created a feeling of confidence in knowing that regardless of the problems facing me, the team is ready and willing to help.

I am confident that through Multiple Management we are building a team that will be hard to beat, and in closing I say to you, Mr. McCormick, and to you, Mr. McGrath and Mr. Murphy, thanks for Multiple Management.

G. W. Denges

R. L. HERRMANN

Rank-and-File Capacities

Blueprint Boy	July, 1935-December, 1935
Heating Installation Draftsman	January, 1936-January, 1937
Clerk and Sales Correspondent— Dealer Sales Department	January, 1937-December, 1937

Management Capacities

Supervisor Application Engineering Department	January, 1938-December, 1938
Assistant Sales Manager—Dealer Sales Department	January, 1939-April, 1942
Assistant Chief Engineer — War Production	May, 1942-June, 1944
Production Control Manager — Aircraft Division	June, 1944-July, 1945
Director Supervisory Training	July, 1945-December, 1946
Manager Industrial Relations	December, 1946-May, 1947
Controller	May, 1947 to present

Board Service

Elected to Junior Board June, 1939—served until June, 1948
Elected to Factory Board June, 1948—still serving

TRUSTEE—The Williamson Heater Company Employees' Trust—
January 3, 1947—still serving
Present Age . . . 34

You know it is quite a task to try to cover in a few minutes
just what Multiple Management has meant to me. It is so
entwined in my short business life that it is impossible to outline briefly or to enumerate the many things that this type of
management has offered not only to me but to everyone of
our supervisory group. It is my feeling that it is true not only
of myself as an individual but that we as a group have been
given many opportunities that do not normally fall to the lot
of people like ourselves in the typical organizations of today.

You know management ideology is traditionally one of
authority and the official leaders of any organization at all
levels are normally expected to be bosses. That's what makes
Multiple Management so different.

The very democratic pattern of leadership of Multiple
Management requires the abandonment of this idea of one
way edict, the take it or leave it philosophy which seems to be
the essence of bossing. As Mr. Kise remarked to me the other
day, Multiple Management is a hard taskmaster—one that not
only permits each of us to exercise our native ability to the
fullest but also goes so far as to see that we take advantage of
this permission and rewards us accordingly.

It calls to mind what St. Paul said in Second Corinthians—
our hope is steadfast knowing that as we are partakers of the
sufferings so shall we be also of the consolation. Multiple
Management is a hard taskmaster—it forces us to keep on the
ball but it also offers many consolations.

So if I were to attempt to point out the one greatest benefit
that I have received from Multiple Management, I perhaps
would choose something that has meant much to me personally, and if many of you will search your conscious and

subconscious mind you will find, I believe, that it has meant much to you.

It is the measure of relief from the frustrations of vocal paralysis that I have felt through the increase in my vocality. Many of us, and particularly myself, are still not too logically articulate, but we can and do find the words and the ability to give voice to our thoughts regardless of the clarity with which they may or may not be expressed. The desire to talk is present in all of us and the lack of the feeling of freedom to express our thoughts is, I believe, responsible for many of the heartaches and social upheavals in our world today.

Multiple Management has not and cannot be expected to develop orators—impressive speakers. I don't think that is its intent but it has made it possible for me to express in somewhat of an understandable manner, some of my ideas, hopes or desires—something that my very nature, prior to and during the early stages of Multiple Management in our company literally shrunk from or cried out against.

This release is a result of the knowledge I have been able to acquire from you, my friends—a knowledge that most persons will, yes are most anxious to be of help to those of us who need help—that people are by nature and compulsion normally kind and considerate.

Multiple Management, like our Republic, when worked at, when truly practiced so that each man or woman feels that he is truly a part, has truly a voice in its operations, has much to offer. It must, however, recognize not only the will of the majority but the needs and interest of the minority. It must not—to succeed—be guilty as some believe many governments have been and are, of being practiced autocratically or used as a front for the advancement of special interest in the guise of a democratic activity.

Yes, were I to point out the greatest personal good that

I have gotten from Multiple Management, I believe I would say a better understanding of my fellow men and the resultant freedom of self-expression.

It is an approach, I believe, to one of the greatest needs of the world today—the advancement of our social skills, the ability to interpret the desires, hopes, ambitions, dreams, needs and dislikes of our fellow men; the art of conversation, if you please, and the improvement in the skills needed to direct these interests to the good of our group or country as a whole; essentially the ability to get along with each other— to realize that every human has individual likes and dislikes —the desire to be an individual and be treated and accepted as such.

In the press of business these things are often overlooked. Our Multiple Management can be the means by which we are kept conscious of this need. It can be the appreciation of the fact that a person can be different from ourselves but more important still the acceptance of his right to be different.

R. L. Herrmann

Gus Leytze

Rank-and-File Capacities

    Order Department Clerk ....March, 1924-June, 1926
    Order Department Senior Clerk ...June, 1926-May, 1928
    Sales Service Correspondent ......June, 1928-December, 1930

Management Capacities

    Supervisor Repair Parts Sales and
      Service Department ....January, 1931-December, 1935
    Supervisor—Order Department ...January, 1936-June, 1937
    Manager Mail Order Sales and
      Supervisor Order Department ...June, 1937-April, 1942
    Manager Production Control, War
      Production ....May, 1942-December, 1942
    Manager—Armor Plate Division ..January, 1943-May, 1944

General Factory Manager—Cin-
cinnati Plant . . . . .June, 1944-March, 1947
General Works Manager — all
plants . . . . .March, 1947 to date

Board Service

Elected to Junior Board December, 1938—served until June, 1942
Elected to Factory Board June, 1942—served until April, 1944
Elected to Senior Board April, 1944—still serving
Elected Vice-President April, 1946—still serving

TRUSTEE—The Williamson Heater Company Employees' Trust—
December, 1941 to April, 1944
Present Age . . . 46

The process of pooled judgment, whereby a group co-
operatively develops pertinent facts and forms balanced conclusions is a technique which, when properly understood and
utilized, can help to reconcile the divergent points of view
inherent in many problems whether they are human problems
or operating problems. That was the first thing I learned during my freshman term in Multiple Management on the Junior
Board which began in 1938.

I learned that the presentation of the facts and the development of the spirit of the pooled judgment process are both
fundamental to the ruling out of prejudice and bias. When
varying points of view are adequately represented, it is usually possible to establish a common set of objectives. When
the entire group is pointed toward these objectives, it becomes
possible to explore the agreements and disagreements within
the group and to expect that the discussion will henceforth
revolve about the facts.

During this early experience I observed our group gradu-
ally learned to dispose of the problems of bias or prejudice
of its own membership by reviewing the facts. After the group

worked together for some time, lapses into bias became less and less frequent.

I think that more than anything else sold me on Multiple Management; I saw in it a vehicle for building co-operation and tolerance. No virtue brings a man more favorably to the attention of those around him, than his willingness to pull his share of the load. When he withholds his co-operation, he at once becomes prominent for his negative attitude and he assuredly becomes unpopular if he allows intolerance to become a dominating characteristic.

I learned from my participation in Multiple Management Board activity five fundamentals for good job management, and over the years I have used them with (in my opinion) good success. 'Course that's only one man's opinion.

The first of these fundamentals is "analysis," or the solving of problems. I learned that before any one can solve a problem of any kind, he needs to have a clear knowledge of the cause or causes of that problem. Otherwise, his efforts to remedy the difficulty represent sheer guess work. That's the manner in which the Boards approach their problems. That became #1 of my five fundamentals for job management.

The second is "planning."

Knowing the cause or causes of the problem, the next step was to determine what could be done to eliminate these causes. Answering this question involved two things: determining what to do, and deciding when, how and by whom it was to be done. So, planning was the second fundamental in which I should become proficient.

The third is "selling ideas." How effectively, for example, boards reacted to a recommendation depended in great measure on how well the members understood and how thoroughly they believed. I realized that I secured results only through my subordinates and as to how effectively my plans were carried out depended on how convincing I could be and how well my subordinates believed in my plans. Therefore, selling ideas became third in my list.

Number four is "follow-through."

Despite the fact that sometimes it took longer to accomplish a task through the medium of a Multiple Management Board, I did recognize that as a result of follow-through or if you prefer follow-up the job did get finished.

The fact that all people are reluctant to change existing habits, and resist new ideas makes it perfectly evident that even though you do the best job in the world of selling an idea or objective you must follow through promptly and consistently if you hope to get that objective realized. Follow-through makes a major contribution to results and is fourth in my list of fundamentals.

The fifth fundamental, developing subordinates, really became important to me ten years ago when working with the Junior Board Sponsorship Program. In my opinion it is most important and is another fundamental in which every supervisor, executive, or manager should be skilled. I think it is one of the gravest weaknesses of industry in general and our own organization can do a far better job in this regard.

I have been privileged to serve the Junior Board, Factory Board, Sales Board and the Senior Board and from each I have been able to add to my store of knowledge. One of the criticisms frequently leveled against Multiple Management or group thinking of any kind is the length of time it consumes. The chairman can do much to minimize waste of time and utilize the efforts of the group most effectively. He must be a good co-ordinator and co-operator. It is his responsibility to keep the issues clear and to center the discussion about them. Especially in discussions concerned with abstract matter, he should stress the objective elements as they are developed.

That I have benefited from my experience with Multiple Management is indisputable, but the reason I did, is, I believe, that it is a continuing, never ending program consistent as a rule by which conduct may be guided. Like truly good planning, it will assure results if properly applied.

Can I say more as to what Multiple Management has done for me?

Gus Leytze

CHAPTER IX

COMMUNISM CAN'T WIN IN THE UNITED STATES—IF!

IF A MAJORITY of American business firms will take active steps to make sure that American workers are proud of and satisfied with their jobs, communism will never gain a sure foothold in the United States.

I am aware of the danger of communism. I have no intention of implying even for a moment that any one of us can relax vigilance against its encroachment. Internationally, communism is a threat to free peoples everywhere. But here in the United States, at least, we have the means at our disposal to stop communism before it gets anywhere in this country—if we will only use them.

Let's begin by examining the kinds of communists as Eric Johnston listed them in his address following his return from Russia in November, 1948. He said:

Broadly speaking, there are at least five types of communists, and perhaps each type could have various subdivisions.

First, there is the Lenin type of communist. These are the doctrinaires, the revolutionists, the fanatics. They are willing to take any risk—any chance—to gain their ends. Such are the men who rule Russia—the members of the Politburo, their commissars and lesser party leaders—their camp followers. They are cold, cynical realists, unswayed by emotion.

Second, there is the intellectual communist. He may be utterly sincere in a faith that communism is all it claims to be. He may, in fact, believe completely that communism is the sheltering arm for the hopeless and the despairing. He is infatuated with the theoretical Utopia he calls communism.

Third, there is the man-against-the-world communist. He may have a personal grievance against the old order; racial discrimination or the childhood memory of injustice to himself or to his family may prompt his conversion. Or, again, he may be merely frustrated by his own inability to move ahead in a democratic world. He may believe that communism will give him the miracle of rebirth.

Fourth, there is the emotionally immature communist. He may be snared by the communist appeal for a brotherhood of man. He may see it as the only way for him to help reform the world. It is possible he revels in the conspiratorial aspect of communism. Or he may simply have gulped the story that communism will inevitably rule the world, and he wants to be on the winning side. Caught young, this type of communist often falls away from the faith as he matures, learns to think for himself and understands that it was duped by false slogans and false promises.

Fifth, there is the stomach communist. He turns to communism in sheer desperation. The fine points of communist ideology mean little or nothing to him. Saving the world means little or nothing to him either. He wants to save himself. He is hungry. The democracy he has known seems to have failed him, and the new and more resounding promises of communism ring aloud in ears which belong to a starving body.

The great rank and file of communists and communist sympathizers in the non-communist world today come in this fifth type— the stomach communist. The worker level is the arena where the main event of Democracy vs. Communism is being fought. . . .

Next, we need to know exactly how communism was born and how it breeds. Its seed grows best in chaos, confusion, and deep dissatisfaction with the existing situation. Communism was the brain child of a mere handful of men who seized control of the world's largest nation and led two hundred million people into the grip of something far more drastic than they ever visualized—all by taking advantage of the emotional upheaval which destroys reason at time of revolution.

In 1917, when medieval Tsarist Russia had collapsed and the Russian army showed signs of cracking, the German Imperial army prepared a sealed baggage car for passage from Switzerland across Germany, into Russia, through a prearranged opening of the German army on its eastern front. In this sealed baggage car the German military officials placed a Russian refugee whose business was to give to the cracking Russian military offensive a final disruptive push from within. His name was Lenin. He was joined in Russia by Trotsky. These two humble servants of the Imperial German Staff accomplished their mission all too well.

Not only did their work, synchronized with the hammer blows of the German army, destroy medieval Russian culture, but by coming thus upon the Russian people with a new and extremely modern idea, defined by the economic philosophy of Karl Marx, it offers one of the most dramatic examples of the way in which an exceedingly technical and systematic theory determines the values, the aims, and the later achievements of a people.

At no time does this influence exhibit itself more dramatically than upon the evening of April 4, 1917, in Finlandsky Station, when, with Trotsky, Lenin stepped off the train in Petrograd. Although the Russians and the Russian army were still fighting the Germans, the revolution has occurred.

The Menshevik communists and the liberal socialists were elated. They accepted the support which they had received from the middle-class democrats as an asset. Nevertheless, according to the dialectic philosophy, not merely of Marx but also of Hegel, the middle-class democratic culture also must be overthrown before the real revolution has occurred.

Consequently, when he stepped off the train, as Trotsky who was present informs us, Lenin, guided as always by this dialectic philosophy of history, did not falter for one moment. Standing on the station platform, he immediately announced, to the great consternation of the Menshevik communists, that they must seize the supreme political power and use it on a socialistic basis.

Six months later the issue between the Menshevik communists who were fighting for socialism by gradual, evolutionary means without an explicit theory to guide them, and Lenin, with his more revolutionary policy prescribed even to the minutest detail over half a century previous by Karl Marx, came to a head. On January, 7,

1918, the All-Russia Central Committee dissolved the elected Constituent Assembly. At last, not merely the Tsar's medieval feudalism but also the traditional modern middle-class bourgeois democracy was liquidated. The dictatorship of the few was a fact.

To be sure, three years more were required for defeat of the counterrevolution from within, which Marx predicted and Lenin expected, . . . Nonetheless, on January 7, 1918, the specified act of history was completed in the precise form and by the precise methods which had been prescribed some seventy-four years earlier in the philosophy of Karl Marx.

But there was an additional complexity in Marx's specifications, about how the revolution must proceed, which Lenin also followed to the minutest detail. The proletariats generally will be in sympathy with the revolution; but, untrained in the Marxian philosophy, they will be in no position to direct the revolution wisely. Consequently, control must be instead in the hands of the few leaders of the Communist party who thoroughly understand the Marxian philosophy. Consequently, when the revolution actually occurs, government will not take on the form of a proletarian democracy; instead, as Marx specifically stated, it will take on a form of dictatorship.

We are now able to understand why Lenin, when he stepped off the train at Finlandsky Station in Petrograd in 1917, refused to accept the democratic revolution as the real revolution.*

Now, having seen how it happened there—can it happen here? It is inconceivable that the American people would ever be allowed under our democratic system to reach the extreme pitch of resentment in the midst of our freedom and abundance that would be necessary to breed a revolution in this country. But people tell me that communism will come upon us, if it does indeed come, not necessarily by revolution but by infiltration and perhaps through political chicanery.

Yet I still maintain that any seeds planted by infiltration, and even politics, must be sown in a deep bed of discontent if they are to grow to such proportions. People who are proud

* From F. S. C. Northrop, *The Meeting of East* and *West*. (New York: The Macmillan Company, 1946.)

of their jobs, their state, their country, put up a tremendous sales resistance to changing that which brought them their good fortune—or present state of being.

The only accurate measure we have of what goes on in the minds of the people of the United States is the evidence presented when the American public speaks its mind in the privacy of the polling place at election time. In the midst of depression the American people by their votes swept Herbert Hoover out of office and brought the Democrats into leadership in American government to bring a change in the way of showing their resentment to existing conditions. In the midst of high employment and long-sustained prosperity in 1948 the people went to the polling places again and upset all the experts by proclaiming, through their votes, that they saw no reason to change conditions.

Our most successful approach, therefore, to the fight against communism in the United States is the positive approach. The only real way to stamp out the threat of communism is through developing an enlightened and publicly accepted free enterprise system. That statement implies two tasks for all of us. Management and labor and government must be close partners in co-operation on this subject.

First, we must research our practices of capitalism, review them analytically, bring them up to date, and arrive at the enlightened capitalism which I believe is that which holds a responsibility for the welfare of people on a par with the responsibility for making a profit.

Secondly, having made sure we are right in our practices of enlightened capitalism, we still have ahead of us the task of gaining widespread public acceptance. People must be told what we are doing, and why they benefit from it.

Each of these tasks is useless without the other. The public cannot be fooled into accepting something which isn't right, and even that which is right is still partially ineffective unless the people know it to be right and accept it accordingly.

Here is a specific five-point program I believe we could follow in America to combat communism:

1. Establish and maintain the proper concept of man's relation to machine. Man is the master of the machine, not its slave. People deserve to be put first in every business consideration.

2. The head of a business is a trustee for all his employees—and not for a favored group of top executives alone. The janitor is just as much a human being as the vice-president and should receive the same consideration of his rights and privileges in the organization as any of his superiors.

3. We can win out together much more easily than we can win out separately. Management, labor, and government face a common enemy in communism. To combat it successfully we must join forces and develop a greater spirit of teamplay than is evidenced by many of the frictions that exist today. Differences of opinion may exist but they should not give rise to bitterness and deep-seated prejudice. Some form of consultative process of shared participation which involves a wide diffusion of knowledge, affirmative consent and creative responsibility by all the members of each corporate team, is essential if democratic ideas are to be translated into democratic action.

4. Education of the new generation beginning in school is an essential. Our students should be taught to understand the American tradition and the positive values to our people of the American way of business as opposed to other systems. We must guard against the infiltration of communists into our educational system. There is no other place where they could do more damage. Similarly, there is no other place where we could do more good than through proper teaching of the young of America.

5. A spiritual reawakening of businessmen to their fundamental responsibilities to God and their fellow men will do as much as anything I know toward correcting injustices and establishing better human relations as the intent of management. Call it ethics, call it religion, call it what you will—the need is great.

It is within the power of management executives in individual business concerns of the United States to accomplish these objectives successfully. There is nothing that government can do or that organized labor unions can do that management cannot do if it only wakes up to its responsibility and takes initiative action—first. We should lead the way.

American industry proved its power in time of crisis during World War II. Here are the facts from the record of production of the United States from 1940 to 1945, as reported in the Twentieth Century Fund Study:

In the five miraculous years, the volume of manufacturing trebled, and the output of raw materials rose 60 per cent. We made 76,000 ships, 315,000 pieces of field artillery, 165,000 naval guns, 86,000 tanks, and 2,400,000 war trucks and half tracks. Of the ships, 64,000 were landing craft, 6,500 were battleships, cruisers, destroyers and other naval vessels, 5,500 were cargo ships, to a total tonnage of 60 million—three times the British merchant fleet which led the world in 1939!

Now comes one of the most extraordinary miracles of all. So furious was our rate of work that we produced *both* guns and butter. America proceeded to turn out guns, yet in 1944 its food output was great enough to keep its armies and allies well supplied, and to give every citizen, on the average, 7 per cent *more* food than in the 1935-1939 period!

We won that war. We can win this one. All we need to do is to accept the inescapable fact that the threat of communism is a crisis just as war is a crisis. Then we must go to work to do something about it. I am convinced we can and will do just that, and that communism can't win in the United States—if we do!

CHAPTER X

THE FUTURE IS BRIGHT

I AM AN optimist about the future of America. In spite of all the signs and portents that look so awesome to some of my business and professional friends, I can't help but believe that we have what it takes to come out on top in the long run.

It seems to me that all of us have a lot to do with that. Our destiny isn't shaped for us—we do the shaping. I doubt that we will arrive at our goal through the effects of any great sweeping legislative acts or government decrees. The future of the country rests still in the same hands that built its past and present—in the combined efforts of all the people who are trying to make things better than they are.

Let's light our light on the hill in our own neighborhood. Enough of these lights will shed their beams about the country to bring a great brilliance to our destiny.

The primary purpose of the management of the future will be to build men. It will place the human factor on a par with profit; knowing that if its human organization is constructed of the right kind of material the profit will take care of itself. Under the new management, a business is best equipped to meet any emergency. Its executives have been trained to express every constructive thought that comes to them. Their personal interests are so closely related to the interests of the company that their success in life depends on the success of the business.

There is much we can learn about the present and the future from a study of the past. Many of the principles in Multiple Management and other similar "new" developments in management thinking actually have their roots in the American colonial days.

Profit-sharing, for example, is really nothing new at all. The early business history of America records that when the whaling ships set sail from the New England coast, everyone who participated in the enterprise—the owner, the captain, the crew, and the cabin boy—shared in the dangers and in the rewards. The owner was entitled to his fair return because he took the financial risk, but when the expedition was successful the owner saw to it that those who had a part in making it successful shared the profits of the venture. This hope of return was one of the earliest incentive systems. All who took part had a direct interest in making the expedition a success. The owner who took too large a share of the returns and disregarded the participation of those who worked with him soon found himself without a crew.

The colonial days gave us great statesmen too. Their zeal was for the country—not for their personal interests only. When they wanted a leader then, they sought the best man in the country and he patriotically served. They fought for principles and not for party pledges alone. The places of position were manned by professional men above reproach who felt they were indebted to their nation to pay back a debt of gratitude through public service.

As business and government have grown large we have got away from many of these early ideals which set our nation on the path to greatness. The fact that business became big had as much as anything I know to do with destroying the close personal relationship between proprietor and worker which once was the rule, and now seems to be almost the exception Multiple Management is an attempt to recapture this same sort of relationship and overcome the obstacle of bigness by setting up a system whereby management is extended down the line closer to the rank-and-file employee.

I do not advocate the loss of productive efficiency that would come about should we return to the small village enterprises of colonial days. What I'm saying is that we can retain all the good of bigness, but at the same time avoid the bad features of it from a human relations standpoint, by tuning our management ideas to fit changing times.

I believe Multiple Management can work successfully in any business of any size. We have seen it succeed in companies with no more than a hundred employees. We have seen it succeed also in companies with many thousands of employees. The question is merely one of adjusting the mechanics or series of boards to fit the needs of the business. The philosophy is still the same philosophy of the small colonial business— to extend management so close to the worker that the two understand one another and work together as a team.

Thus far I have been talking principally in terms of the business community, but of course business is only a part of the framework of America. An increasingly important part, and one which is more and more closely interrelated with the business community, is government—federal, state, and local. Businessmen should take a more active and direct interest in government than they have shown to date. Their responsibilities extend not only to people as employees, but also to people as citizens.

This nation discovered the power of its people in 1932, 1936, 1940, 1944, but more particularly on the morning of November 3, 1948. For weeks the nation had listened to political experts. Every so-called public opinion poll was emphatic, decisive. Magazines and newspapers long heralded as molders of public opinion were flatly positive in their predictions.

And yet, on November 2, the people of the United States went to the polls and showed their power. They elected as president of the United States the man the experts had marked for certain defeat. Never underestimate the power of people in voting—or in the plants, factories, or homes of the nation. More and more their voice will be listened to.

Here is a lesson that no one should forget. After all, who runs a democratic country? An influential few—or the people?

Now we know. Both perhaps, but the final curtain can be lifted or rung down by the final vote of its people.

This new evidence didn't strengthen my belief alone, but few of us in business know and understand what the great majority of people in America really think. In a way, many of us are planning and operating in a vacuum. We listen to a few advisers, gauge the reactions of other people much like ourselves who are closest to us day after day, and proceed more or less blindly along paths which may or may not be the ones the people are following. For example, too many bankers and industrialists associate with their own clique exclusively. Too many labor men only travel in the company with their own clique. America is bigger and we must know the other side if we will be successful in private enterprise— and keep this nation free.

And yet our very existence depends on what the people want. They are the customers for our merchandise and at the same time the employees who man our production lines and market our goods. They are the great American public whose favor may lead us to prosperity and whose disfavor and lack of patronage may cause our sales to drop, our costs to rise, and our profits to disappear.

They even determine the business system under which we operate. Business systems are determined by governments, and governments are determined by the people. Governments are people. Business is people.

That is why Multiple Management and all human relations philosophies like it should now be extended to the area of government—just as they have been successfully applied during the past seventeen years to the field of business.

A business concern can no more hold itself remote from government in the United States today than the United States as a nation can hold itself remote from the other nations of the world. Time and transportation have beaten down the barriers. We are thoroughly interrelated and the process of dissolving the mixture is as intricate as that of splitting the atom into its component parts. In the modern complex nation we know today, where does the force of government and that of business begin? Who can draw the fine line of separation? Where does management stop and labor begin—are we not actually all laborers—but some the managers?

Who runs most governments, anyway? The people, of course. But because the people are frequently apathetic about going to the polls and registering their opinions, particularly in primary elections, the actual control of many local, state, and national offices is in the hands of a class of people who care little about business and its objectives.

We need business-minded statesmen in government for the protection of American free competitive enterprise.

Every sizable company has among its executive personnel men who would make competent public officials. Most of these men, because of their business training and experience in efficient methods of operation, would be superior to the average professional politician who holds the average public office. He would be more honest, direct, and less selfish to his own personal interests.

A few unsung heroes have crossed the line from business into government, and because there have been so few the fact usually makes headlines and arouses wonder throughout the community. They are usually praised by their associates, damned by their career men colleagues in government, and held up by the public as a sort of curiosity.

It will be necessary for honest, zealous, competent young men in business to become interested in being elected to local offices, and for experienced businessmen to accept candidacies for higher positions. The young men should learn politics the hard way from the ground up as they learn business. Government and politics are a part of our pattern of life. Service in this field is as much a part of the duty of young men, in my opinion, as service in time of military emergency. After all, warfare is a bloody business and people get killed. In politics, we have some evidence of dirty business and people who enter public life must be prepared to accept the sacrifices of living in the goldfish bowl of public scrutiny.

The fact that many businessmen have already given bountifully and faithfully of their time and money in the interests of building up better government goes without saying, but I believe we should do more. Those of us who cannot go into government directly can surely find or help competent substitutes among the younger men of our business. We should support them to protect our way of life in America. Each of us owes a debt to work to the fullest of our capacity to make the community in which we live the most successful place we know. Only in that way can we stabilize and build a greater nation.

This book is written as a challenge to young businessmen,

and to young Americans. Business is a vital force in this country and can forever remain so, but not without great sacrifices. That calls for better human relations, for applying the principles of the "dignity of man" to all mankind, particularly laboring man, through researching and keeping up with the constant change of things.

There is nothing wrong with America that cannot be overcome by the oncoming generation of young men who have the courage, tolerance, and patience and the ability to take the great lessons of liberty and freedom that we have learned and use them as a platform with which to go on to greater heights. This generation is the trustee of our traditions, our heritage, and our liberty.

To these young men I would urge that they prepare themselves now for that which will be required of them when they become leaders of businesses. The new type of businessman in the future must be a student of people. He must understand government and politics and human relations as thoroughly as he understands productive processes, profits, and sales methods. He must be a diplomat because it will require real diplomacy to deal with complex legal and human factors of the future.

The veterans of World War II offer the finest prospects for this newer type of businessmen and statesmen. They know more about the world as a whole because of the tools we have invented in the past. They have seen much of the world and understand it better than past generations did. They can accomplish more and quicker because of the improved transportation and communication methods. The airplane has shortened distance and television has brought the world into our living rooms at the moment of the action.

Perhaps it is just as well that a newer generation should

take over perplexing problems that may have our elder statesmen and elder businessmen baffled today. Perhaps our older
men have so crystallized their views toward unions and laws
and other opposing forces that they cannot possibly meet with
clear judgment around a conference table as a team. Prejudice
inevitably affects the decisions of mature men more than those
of younger men.

Life has a way of giving each generation a job to do and
then turning the same torch of freedom over to be protected
by another generation. In my opinion, the most valuable concept we of today's world will turn over to the generation to
follow us is our growing knowledge of the art and science of
working with people. We are learning to put men above machines. We are studying the needs and wants of human beings
and are beginning to minister to them in management with a
sincere interest in the welfare of our workers. Call it religion,
call it human relations in business, call it anything you desire,
but I am sure of one thing: our future will reach its greatest
brilliance only as we improve our social arts to catch up with
science; in order that physical progress may be matched by
an even more important human progress.

Thomas Alva Edison said just this when he was asked one
time: "Mr. Edison, what do you think will be the greatest
invention of the next generation?"

Mr. Edison replied: "Well, I have often thought about that
myself. I doubt a good deal if it will be along mechanical
lines. You will be surprised to hear me say this, but I sort of
feel that it will be along psychological or spiritual lines. I
sort of feel that somebody, sometime, is going to invent something which will get people to have the right point of view
toward life. That is what America is waiting for today, and

only that will solve her problems and reduce the cost of living."*

I wonder if the creation of the new science of human relations is not, indeed, that greatest invention which Thomas Edison predicted.

The invention is there for the virile youth of our new generation to use. The greatest of all inventions is in good hands. The future is bright—for the power of good people is atomic.

* From an address by Roger W. Babson, Chicago, January 30, 1920.

APPENDICES

APPENDIX A

JUNIOR AND FACTORY BOARD RATING FORM

In actual use, the form illustrated on the following double-page spread is an 8½- by 11-inch printed sheet. The rating blocks and the heading "McCormick & Company, Inc., Junior and Factory Board Rating Form" appear on one side, and the "Instructions" and "General Directions for Using the Rating Form" which are given below on the other.

INSTRUCTIONS

1. Prior to rating, reread "General Directions for Using the Rating Form" printed below.
2. Rate objectively—compare individuals rated to described traits (descriptions) and not to other individuals.
3. In rating use all knowledge you have of an individual including (but not restricted to) Junior or Factory Board activity, with this single exception—exclude technical knowledge or technical characteristics and do not attempt to evaluate technical skill.
4. Rate frankly, remembering that too lax use of high ratings is unfair to the man who most conspicuously earned highest ratings.
5. If in any isolated case you find it impossible to use definitions, state reasons on reverse of rating form.

GENERAL DIRECTIONS FOR USING THE RATING FORM

1. Be fair. Rating a man is serious business. Hurried and unjustified ratings are likely to jeopardize another man's reputation and welfare. Take enough time to arrive at considered (not snap) judgments and thereby be fair to yourself and your responsibilities as well as to the other fellow.
2. Be objective. Ratings should be done in a purely objective, factual, impersonal manner. Let your judgments, supported by facts and observations, not your feelings, be the basis of your ratings. Personal considerations have no place in judging another.

97

McCormick & Company, Inc.
JUNIOR AND FACTORY BOARD RATING FORM

RATING OF................ BY................ DATE................

	E	D	C	B	A	POINTS
HUMAN RELATIONS — Consider: The 'spirit of Multiple Management' as reflected in and applied to human relations; understanding of people; consideration for others; tact in dealing with people without giving offense; ability to "bring out the best" in others.	Generally self-centered, tactless and inconsiderate of others; occasionally exhibits misunderstanding of others; actions and speech occasionally offend	Occasionally disregards feelings of others; occasionally; exhibits misunderstanding of others; lowers morale of group; gives appearance of disregarding interests and welfare of others	Generally considerate, tactful and understanding but occasionally fails.	Usually considerate, understanding and tactful; sets welfare of others above self; handles others well; rarely offends	Consistently shows consideration and understanding of others; furthers their best interests; tactful in dealing with all at all times; rarely offends; consistently practices Multiple Management; inspires others.	....
VISION — Consider: The ability to foresee future conditions and long-term effect of present actions; the ability to suggest action affecting a long-term program.	Rarely foresees the future; thinks in terms of the present and only occasionally recognizes the long-term program.	Generally thinks in terms of the present but occasionally can recognize the long-term program.	Usually recognizes the long-term program; generally thinks in terms of future.	Usually foresees a long-term program and generally thinks in terms of future conditions and long-term effect of present actions.	Consistently alert in developing new ideas for a long-term program; thinks in terms of future conditions and actions, understands effect of present actions on long-term program.	....
INITIATIVE — Consider: The ability to see what needs to be done; to start action by seeking counsel of others concerned; a self-starter; ability to follow through despite obstacles.	Rarely makes suggestions and needs considerable help in starting action; usually stopped by obstacles.	Occasionally able to see what needs to be done; may contribute one or two ideas of a minor nature; finds it difficult to get started.	Generally detects ideas and starts action with reasonable promptness; occasionally stopped by obstacles	Usually detects and hunts for ideas and starts action promptly; generally carries programs beyond obstacles.	Consistently quick to hunt for and detect ideas, constantly prompt in seeking action, constantly makes suggestions for immediate action and carries program over obstacles.	....

Trait	Rating 1	Rating 2	Rating 3	Rating 4	Rating 5	
JUDGMENT Consider: The ability to analyze a situation thoroughly and after careful consideration to make sound decisions; ability to recognize the difference between the important and the trivial; ability to use wisdom and common sense and make sound decisions in emergencies and under pressure.	Generally jumps to conclusions and overlooks important factors; usually illogical in thinking and generally gives too much importance to the trivial.	Occasionally makes sound judgments; has difficulty in differentiating between the important and the trivial; Occasionally makes poor decision under pressure.	Generally reaches a sound decision but occasionally overlooks important factors.	Usually logical in proposing the solution, usually makes sound judgments; has good sense of values.	Consistently makes sound judgments under all conditions, coordinates thinking and analyzes soundly; makes sound decisions with speed when necessary.	··········
COOPERATIVENESS Consider: Ability to work with others wholeheartedly and effectively; readiness and willingness to give new ideas and suggestions a fair trial; follows through voluntarily; a team player.	Rarely has a desire to cooperate; occasionally a "knocker"; is apt to think negatively on programs of others.	Usually cooperates reluctantly; needs some pressure to follow through; generally a "lone wolf" rather than a team worker.	Accepts assignments but occasionally fails to follow through.	Accepts his share of team assignments and follows through; usually works with others effectively, accepts programs of others.	Consistently goes out of way to assist others; excellent team worker; follows through to completion; gives others' programs an enthusiastic trial.	··········
POISE Consider: Self-confidence; the ability to assume the attitude of success; the ability to remain confident and poised and optimistic under trying or varying circumstances; ability to remain calm and steady under pressure; ability to give and take criticism impersonally; even-tempered; ability to put others at ease.	Quick-tempered; easily aroused; rarely at ease; tends to make personal issue of business problems.	Usually self-conscious; loses control under pressure.	Usually confident but often shows strain under pressure.	Generally self-controlled; usually confident but occasionally shows strain under pressure.	Consistently confident and calm and steady under pressure; considers situations impersonally.	··········

TOTAL .. ..

Some raters tend to be too critical while others tend to be too lenient. Remember that your ratings reflect the accuracy of your judgments; if you are biased, prejudiced, or unduly influenced by others, it will show up in your rating forms. Be independent of any influence or prejudice; do not consult anyone in making your judgments.

3. Rate all persons on a single quality first; then proceed by rating all persons on the second quality, then the third, etc. This focuses the rater's attention on a particular quality rather than a particular individual. Hence, every other quality is disregarded but the one being rated. In this manner you try to avoid the chief weakness inherent in rating—that of allowing a single characteristic to color one's judgment on all other factors. Remember, many ratings are rendered useless simply because a rater has permitted a general favorable or unfavorable impression that he has formed of a person to guide his thinking in rating him on several more or less independent qualities.

4. Keep a small notebook in which to record unusual occurrences to refresh your memory and to justify your ratings. Very briefly record all favorable or unfavorable incidents, dated, in connection with any particular individual and the traits involved. If a person has impressed you with having exercised unusual vision, initiative, poise, etc., during a board meeting, record the incident before you forget it; if he exhibited unusually poor judgment or human relations, etc., record it. Do not make this recording a cumbersome task. Consider every man average in every trait until your evidence shows that you are justified in rating him higher or lower. Review all entries made in your notebook for this purpose.

5. Human beings are subject to change; they do not "stay put." Consequently, it is not good procedure to consult former ratings of an individual while you are in the process of rating him again. Each rating should be an entirely new appraisal of the individual. Judge each person on his actual accomplishments during each rating period.

6. When you have prepared yourself to make a careful and unbiased appraisal in accordance with the foregoing principles:
    1. For each category (Human Relations, Vision, etc.) on the rating form, determine into which of the major subdivi-

sions (a, b, c, d, e) the individual's performance places him.

2. Put a checkmark in the space, which, in your opinion, is the level of the individual's performance WITHIN this subdivision.

3. Do NOT total or consider numerical evaluation.

BYLAWS OF THE JUNIOR BOARD OF EXECUTIVES
MCCORMICK & COMPANY, INC.
REVISED AND ADOPTED AS OF JUNE 5, 1947

ARTICLE I

NAME, PURPOSE

SECTION 1. The name of this board shall be "The Junior Board of Executives."

SECTION 2. It shall be the purpose of this board with the Senior Board and other management boards to manage McCormick & Co., Inc.; to provide opportunity for junior executives and young men of potential ability to participate in the management of McCormick & Co., Inc.; to provide a clearing house for their ideas and a forum for expression of their opinions in management; to train and educate them in over-all company operations.

ARTICLE II

MEMBERSHIP

SECTION 1. All executive, administrative or professional employees of McCormick & Co., Inc., and its subsidiaries, and all employees showing potential ability in these classifications as determined by scientific rating charts shall be eligible for membership provided, however, they are not members of the stockholder-elected Senior Board of Directors. Membership shall consist of two classifications: Regular and Associate.

SECTION 2. Regular membership is limited to twelve *regular* members, who shall be executive, administrative, or professional employees of the company.

SECTION 3. Associate membership is limited to eight *associate* members. These must be executive, administrative, or professional employees of the company; or employees who show potential ability in these classifications as determined by scientific rating charts. Any associate member becomes eligible for consideration for regular membership upon completion of four three-month terms within twenty-four months, or upon being rated to the Membership Committee. Associates shall have full membership rights except the right to vote or hold office. Associates shall participate in rating members at the semi-annual ratings.

SECTION 4. Ratings for regular members are conducted during the first week in January and the first week in July each year in the following manner: Each member (regular and associate) of the board prepares a merit rating of every member of the board except himself on an approved merit rating chart provided for that purpose, to be returned to a member of the Senior Board for tabulation. The six highest rated members automatically become the Membership Committee. The names of those not rated to the Membership Committee must be placed in nomination, together with all other eligible candidates. The Membership Committee then appoints the additional members.

SECTION 5. From a list of those eligible, associate members shall be appointed by the regular members quarterly at special meetings to be called the first week in January, April, July and October.

SECTION 6. Three members, including at least one regular and one associate, must be dropped from the board at each semi-annual rating. At least one regular member, rating below the first six at a semi-annual rating and who has served two consecutive years on the Junior Board as a regular member, is not eligible for re-appointment for the ensuing six-month term.

ARTICLE III

MEETINGS

SECTION 1. There shall be at least two regularly scheduled meetings each month in the Junior Board of Executives room or in such other place as the chairman may designate.

SECTION 2. Additional meetings may be called by the chairman or the Executive Committee at any time when considered necessary. At no time should there be more than a two-week lapse between meetings.

SECTION 3. Appointment meetings, as provided in Article II, shall be called the first week in January, April, July, and October of each year.

SECTION 4. Failure of any member to attend as many as two consecutive regularly scheduled meetings will be considered sufficient lack of participation to make that member liable to be dropped from the board. A successor may be appointed by the board to fill the unexpired term of the member dropped.

SECTION 5. An attendance of a majority of regular members shall constitute a quorum at any meeting.

SECTION 6. All meetings of the board shall be conducted informally, with parliamentary procedure applying on voting and order of business.

SECTION 7. All recommendations to the Senior Board must be unanimously passed. Any recommendation on which a unanimous agreement cannot be reached will go on the minutes and be held for further consideration.

SECTION 8. Unanimous recommendations of the Junior Board are subject to the approval of the Senior Board. It is the responsibility of the chairman, with the Executive Committee of the Junior Board, to review all unanimous recommendations with the Senior Board and report its decisions at the following meeting.

ARTICLE IV

COMMITTEES

SECTION 1. The three highest rated regular members at each semi-annual rating with exception of the officers shall constitute the Executive Committee for each term. The Executive Committee shall have power to delegate authorities of officership to a regular member of the group temporarily in the absence of the chairman and secretary.

SECTION 2. The six members receiving the highest ratings at the semi-annual rating shall constitute the Membership Committee for the ensuing term. The Membership Committee shall have power to appoint the regular members to the board.

ARTICLE V

OFFICERS

Section 1.   A chairman and secretary shall be elected at the first regular meeting after the quarterly appointment to serve for a three-month term of office. Both nominations and elections for these offices shall be made by separate written ballot by the regular members.

Section 2.   The chairman shall be the chief executive officer of this board. He shall preside at all meetings; shall have general supervision and direction of other officers and committees and shall be an ex-officio member of all standing committees. He shall have all powers and authorities usually vested in the office of chairmanship.

Section 3.   The secretary shall keep the records of the board, give proper notice to the members of all meetings of the group, and perform such other duties as may be prescribed from time to time by the chairman. He shall record votes and minutes of the proceedings of all meetings in a book kept for that purpose. In the absence of the chairman, the secretary shall preside and have all the powers vested in the office of chairman.

ARTICLE VI

AMENDMENTS

Section 1.   These bylaws may be amended only by unanimous vote of a quorum present at any meeting, provided the amendment has been posted for the complete membership for a two-week period.

BYLAWS OF THE FACTORY BOARD OF EXECUTIVES

MCCORMICK & COMPANY, INC.
REVISED AND ADOPTED AS OF JANUARY 3, 1947

ARTICLE I

NAME, PURPOSE

SECTION 1. The name of this board shall be "The Factory Board of Executives."

SECTION 2. It shall be the purpose of this board with the Senior Board and other management boards to manage McCormick & Co., Inc.; to provide opportunity for factory executives and young men of potential ability to participate in the management of McCormick & Co., Inc.; to provide a clearinghouse for their ideas and a forum for expression of their opinions in management; to train and educate them in over-all company operations.

ARTICLE II

MEMBERSHIP

SECTION 1. All executive, administrative, or professional employees of McCormick & Co., Inc., and its subsidiaries, and all employees showing potential ability in these classifications as determined by scientific rating charts shall be eligible for membership provided, however, they are not members of the stockholder-elected Senior Board of Directors. Membership shall consist of two classifications: Regular and Associate.

SECTION 2. Regular membership is limited to twelve *regular* members, who shall be executive, administrative, or professional employees of the company.

SECTION 3. Associate membership is limited to eight *associate* members. These must be executive, administrative, or professional employees of the company; or employees who show potential ability in these classifications as determined by scientific rating charts. Any associate member becomes eligible for consideration for regular membership upon completion of four three-month terms within twenty-four months, or upon being rated to the Membership Committee. Associates shall have full membership rights except the right to vote or hold office. Associates shall participate in rating members at the semi-annual ratings.

Section 4. Ratings for regular members are conducted during the first week of May and the first week of November each year in the following manner: Each member (regular and associate) of the board prepares a merit rating of every member of the board except himself on an approved merit rating chart provided for that purpose, to be returned to a member of the Senior Board for tabulation. The six highest rated members automatically become the Membership Committee. The names of those not rated to the Membership Committee must be placed in nomination, together with all other eligible candidates. The Membership Committee then appoints the additional members.

Section 5. From a list of those eligible, associate members shall be appointed by the regular members quarterly at special meetings to be called the first week in February, May, August, and November.

Section 6. Three members, including at least one regular and one associate, must be dropped from the board at each semi-annual rating. At least one regular member, rating below the first six at a semi-annual rating and who has served two consecutive years on the Factory Board as a regular member, is not eligible for re-appointment for the ensuing six-month term.

ARTICLE III

MEETINGS

Section 1. There shall be at least two regularly scheduled meetings each month in the Factory Board of Executives room or in such other place as the chairman may designate.

Section 2. Additional meetings may be called by the chairman or the Executive Committee at any time when considered necessary.

At no time should there be more than a two-week lapse between meetings.

SECTION 3. Appointment meetings, as provided in Article II, shall be called the first week in February, May, August, and November of each year.

SECTION 4. Failure of any member to attend as many as four consecutive regularly scheduled meetings will be considered sufficient lack of participation to make that member liable to be dropped from the board. A letter of comment and suggestion from an absent member should be considered as participation in board activities. A successor may be appointed by the board to fill the unexpired term of the member dropped.

SECTION 5. An attendance of a majority of regular members shall constitute a quorum at any meeting.

SECTION 6. All meetings of the board shall be conducted informally, with parliamentary procedure applying on voting and order of business.

SECTION 7. All recommendations to the Senior Board must be unanimously passed. Any recommendation on which a unanimous agreement cannot be reached will go on the minutes and be held for further consideration.

SECTION 8. Unanimous recommendations of the Factory Board are subject to the approval of the Senior Board. It is the responsibility of the chairman, with the Executive Committee of the Factory Board, to review all unanimous recommendations with the Senior Board and report its decisions at the following meeting.

ARTICLE IV

COMMITTEES

SECTION 1. The three highest rated regular members at each semi-annual rating, with the exception of the officers, shall constitute the Executive Committee for each term. The Executive Committee shall have power to delegate authorities of officership to a regular member of the group temporarily in the absence of the chairman and secretary.

SECTION 2. The six members receiving the highest ratings at the semi-annual rating shall constitute the Membership Committee for the ensuing term. The Membership Committee shall have power to appoint the regular members to the board.

ARTICLE V

OFFICERS

SECTION 1.   A chairman and a secretary shall be elected at the first regular meeting after the quarterly appointment to serve for a three-month term of office. Both nominations and election for these offices shall be made by separate written ballot by the regular members.

SECTION 2.   The chairman shall be the chief executive officer of this board. He shall preside at all meetings; shall have general supervision and direction of other officers and committees and shall be an ex-officio member of all standing committees. He shall have all powers and authority usually vested in the office of chairmanship.

SECTION 3.   The secretary shall keep the records of the board, give proper notice to the members of all meetings of the group, and perform such other duties as may be prescribed from time to time by the chairman. He shall record votes and minutes of the proceedings of all meetings in a book kept for that purpose. In the absence of the chairman, the secretary shall preside and have all the powers vested in the office of chairman.

ARTICLE VI

AMENDMENTS

SECTION 1.   These bylaws may be amended only by unanimous vote of a quorum present at any meeting, provided the amendment has been posted for the complete membership for a two-week period.

APPENDIX D

BYLAWS OF THE SALES BOARD

MCCORMICK & COMPANY

ARTICLE I

NAME, PURPOSE

SECTION 1. Name:

The name of this organization shall be "The Sales Board of Directors of McCormick & Co., Inc."

SECTION 2. Purpose:

It shall be the purpose of this organization to provide participation of salesmen and sales executives in the McCormick plan of Multiple Management to educate them in company operations; to give them a clearinghouse for their ideas and to secure the benefit of their sales experience in management.

ARTICLE II

MEMBERSHIP

SECTION 1. Number:

The membership of this organization shall consist of ten outside sales representatives of McCormick & Co. and five executives in the Baltimore office of the company. These are to be considered as active members. In addition, there shall be five associate members chosen from the outside sales organization.

SECTION 2. Election of Outside Members:

The ten outside members shall be elected at the first semi-annual meeting of the Sales Board, which will be called as close to January 1st of each year as practical.

110

The Election Committee shall be composed of the Executive Committee and the corresponding secretary, and one additional outside member appointed by the Executive Committee. They shall elect the ten board members for the ensuing year, who will be selected from a list of twenty nominees submitted by the Sales Department—which automatically includes the ten current outside active and five associate members—with the best sales and merchandising record and contribution to the company's welfare.

At least three of the ten outside active members must be replaced by new members, who have not served as active members during the past year, at each annual election. Any active member not returned to the Sales Board in an annual election must be included in the list of nominees proposed by the Sales Department for the next annual election. However, he should normally continue to serve as a member of the committee on which he was active during his membership on the board for the ensuing year.

SECTION 3.   Election of Associate Members:

At the same time, the Election Committee shall elect five associate outside members chosen from a selected list of prospects submitted by the Sales Department on the basis of achievement. These associate members shall have the privilege of attending all meetings of the Sales Board and entering into all discussions, but shall not have the power to vote.

SECTION 4.   Inside Members:

The five inside members, chosen from executives in the Baltimore office of the company who are not actively serving on the Senior Board of Directors, shall be appointed each year by the Senior Board of Directors.

SECTION 5.   Honorary Membership:

Honorary membership on the Sales Board is extended with all privileges to the president of McCormick & Co., Inc. The meetings of the Sales Board and its committees shall be open to him and all members of the Senior Board at any time, and he may authorize any employee at his discretion to attend meetings ex officio and receive the benefit of any, with full privileges of expression. Authority is vested in the president or by three-fourths majority vote of the board to remove any member for justifiable cause.

SECTION 6. Vacancies:

In the event of a vacancy's occurring on the board among the outside members during the year, the Election Committee, as set forth in Article I, Section 4, shall ballot on a list of nominees to be submitted by the Sales Department to select a replacement member to serve the balance of the term until the next election. A vacancy occurring among inside members shall be filled by Senior Board appointment.

ARTICLE III

MEETINGS

SECTION 1. Meetings:

The Sales Board shall meet in Baltimore or elsewhere at times to be determined at the discretion of the Sales Board and Executive Committee, but not less than twice annually.

SECTION 2. Meeting Notification:

The secretary shall notify each member in writing at least fourteen days in advance of meeting dates.

SECTION 3. Quorum:

An attendance of ten members shall constitute a quorum for any meeting provided that at least six outside members are present.

SECTION 4. Order of Business:

Roll call
Report on actions on recommendations of preceding meeting
Committee reports and recommendations
Unfinished business
New business
Election of officers for the ensuing year.

SECTION 5. Voting:

All recommendations and resolutions must be adopted by unanimous vote and, before becoming a part of the company's policies, must be approved by the Senior Board of Directors or the department head.

SECTION 6. Suggestions:

The entire sales organization will be duly notified in advance of each Sales Board meeting so that they may send suggestions, recommendations and ideas to committee chairmen or members.

ARTICLE IV

OFFICERS

SECTION 1. Officers:

The officers of the Sales Board shall be a chairman, vice chairman, secretary, and corresponding secretary. They shall be elected at the first semi-annual meeting to serve for a full-year term. The chairman and the vice chairman shall be elected from the outside membership; the secretary and corresponding secretary from the inside membership.

SECTION 2. Chairman:

The chairman shall be the chief executive officer. He shall preside at all meetings; shall appoint and direct the work of the committees, and shall have an ex-officio membership on all committees. He shall have all further powers and authority usually vested in the office of chairman.

SECTION 3. Vice Chairman:

In the event of the absence of the chairman of the board, the vice chairman will take over and if during the year a vacancy should occur in the office of chairman, the vice chairman will preside and finish the term of office for that year.

SECTION 4. Secretary:

The secretary shall keep the records; notify the members of meetings; issue minutes of meetings; send and receive ballots in the event of elections by mail, and record all votes and proceedings in a book kept for that purpose. He shall perform such other duties of the office as may be prescribed from time to time by the chairman.

SECTION 5.   Corresponding Secretary:

The corresponding secretary shall keep members advised by mail, in the interim between meetings, of committee reports, resolutions, and other matters requiring correspondence on Sales Board matters. He shall perform such other duties of his office as may be prescribed from time to time by the chairman. Votes by mail should clear through the chairman of the Sales Board.

ARTICLE V

COMMITTEES

SECTION 1.   Executive Committee:

The Executive Committee shall be composed of the chairman and a committee of four or more appointed by the chairman to meet at intervals as required between regular Sales Board meetings. Recommendations and findings of this committee are to be submitted to entire membership of Sales Board for final approval and subsequent recommendations to management.

SECTION 2.   Chairmanship of Committees:

The chairman shall appoint each member a chairman of a designated committee as may be needed to carry on the work of the Sales Board on all matters relating to sales and merchandising operations.

ARTICLE VI

AMENDMENTS

SECTION 1.

These bylaws may be amended only by unanimous vote of a quorum present at any meeting.

APPENDIX E

BYLAWS OF THE INSTITUTIONAL SALES BOARD OF EXECUTIVES

ARTICLE I

NAME, PURPOSE

SECTION 1. Name:

The name of this group shall be "The Institutional Sales Board of Executives" of McCormick & Company, Inc.

SECTION 2. Purpose:

It shall be the purpose of this Institutional Sales Board of Executives to provide for participation of Institutional Salesmen and Institutional Sales Executives in the McCormick plan of Multiple Management; to educate them in company operations; to give them a clearinghouse for their ideas; and to transmit the benefit of their institutional sales experience to management.

ARTICLE II

MEMBERSHIP

SECTION 1. Number:

The membership of this Institutional Sales Board of Executives shall consist of six institutional sales representatives of McCormick & Company, Inc., operating outside of the plants; and two executives operating within the company's plants. These eight persons are to be considered regular members. In addition, there shall be two associate members also chosen from the institutional sales representatives operating outside of the plants.

SECTION 2.   Appointment of Regular Members:

The six regular members operating outside of the plants shall be appointed at the first semi-annual meeting of the Institutional Sales Board of Executives which will be called as near to January first of each year as practicable.

The Appointment Committee shall consist of the chairman of the Institutional Sales Board of Executives and those he shall appoint to the Executive Committee; the secretary of the Institutional Sales Board of Executives and additional members who shall be appointed by the above-mentioned Executive Committee as the need arises. The Appointment Committee shall elect the six regular members for the ensuing year, which members will be selected from a list of twelve nominees submitted by the Institutional Sales Department. This list of twelve nominees will consist of those men who have been selected by the Institutional Sales Department as having the best sales records and having made the greatest contributions to the company's welfare.

At specified annual meetings at least two of the six outside regular members must be replaced by new members who have not served as regular members during the past year. Any regular member not re-appointed to the Institutional Sales Board of Executives at an annual meeting for appointments is to be included in the list of nominees proposed by the Institutional Sales Department for the next annual appointing date. However, this member shall continue to serve on the committee until the time he completes the assignment he began at the time he was a regular member of the Institutional Sales Board of Executives.

SECTION 3.   Appointment of Associate Members:

At the same time the six regular members operating outside the plants are appointed, the Appointment Committee shall appoint two associate members who shall be selected from a list of prospects submitted by the Institutional Sales Department. This list of prospects is to be made up of men who have been selected because of their progressiveness and achievements. These associate members shall have the privilege of attending all meetings of the Institutional Sales Board of Executives and entering into all discussions, but shall not have the power to vote.

SECTION 4. Appointment of Executive Members Operating Within the Plants:

Each year two members chosen from executives in the McCormick & Company plants, who are not actively serving on the Senior Board of Directors, shall be appointed by the Senior Board of Directors to the Institutional Sales Board of Executives.

SECTION 5. Honorary Membership:

Honorary membership, with all privileges, to the Institutional Sales Board of Executives is extended to the president of McCormick & Company, Inc. The meetings of the Institutional Sales Board of Executives, as well as those of its committees, shall be open to him as well as to all members of the Senior Board; and the president, at his discretion, may authorize any employee to attend these meetings ex officio with full privileges of expression. Should the cause be justifiable, authority shall be vested in the president and/or in a three-fourths majority vote of the Institutional Sales Board of Executives members to remove a member from the Institutional Sales Board of Executives.

SECTION 6. Vacancies:

In the event a vacancy occurs during the year among the six regular members operating outside of the plants, the Appointment Committee, as set forth in Article I, Section 4, shall appoint from a list of nominees which is to be submitted by the Institutional Sales Department a member to serve until the next appointing date. A vacancy occurring among the executive members shall be filled by Senior Board appointment.

ARTICLE III

MEETINGS

SECTION 1. Meetings:

The Institutional Sales Board of Executives shall meet at places and at times to be determined by the Institutional Sales Board of Executives or the Executive Committee, but the board shall meet not less than twice annually.

SECTION 2.   Meeting Notification:

The secretary shall notify each member in writing at least fourteen days prior to the date set for the meeting.

SECTION 3.   Quorum:

Six members shall constitute a quorum at any meeting provided that at least four members operating outside of the plant are present.

SECTION 4.   Order of Business:
Roll call
Minutes of previous meeting
Report of action on recommendations presented at preceding meeting
Committee reports and recommendations
Unfinished business
New business

SECTION 5.   Voting:

All recommendations and resolutions shall be adopted only after unanimous approval; and, before becoming a part of the company's policies, they shall be approved by either the Senior Board of Directors or heads of the departments concerned.

SECTION 6.   Suggestions:

All of the members of the Institutional Sales Department will be duly notified in advance of each Institutional Sales Board of Executives meeting so that they may send their suggestions, recommendations, and ideas to committee chairmen or members.

ARTICLE IV

OFFICERS

SECTION 1.   Officers:

The officers of the Institutional Sales Board of Executives shall be a chairman and a secretary. They shall be elected at the first semiannual meeting and will serve for a term of one year. The chairman shall be elected from the members operating outside of the plants; and the secretary from the members operating within the plants.

SECTION 2.   Chairman:

The chairman shall be the chief executive officer. He shall preside at all meetings; shall appoint and direct the work of the committees, and shall have an ex-officio membership on all committees. He shall have all further powers and authority usually vested in the office of chairman.

SECTION 3.   Secretary:

The secretary shall keep the records; notify the members of meetings; issue minutes of meetings; and record all proceedings in a book kept for that purpose. He shall perform such other duties of the office as may be prescribed from time to time by the chairman.

ARTICLE V

COMMITTEES

SECTION 1.   Executive Committee:

The Executive Committee shall be composed of the chairman and a committee of three or more members appointed by the chairman to meet at intervals, as required, between regular Institutional Sales Board of Executives' meetings. Recommendations and findings of this Executive Committee shall be submitted to the Institutional Board of Executives for final approval and subsequently recommended to management.

SECTION 2.   Chairmanship of Committees:

The chairman of the Institutional Sales Board of Executives shall appoint each member of the board to a designated committee as may be needed to carry out the work of the Institutional Sales Board of Executives.

ARTICLE VI

AMENDMENTS

SECTION 1.   Amendment of Bylaws:

These bylaws may be amended only by a unanimous vote of a quorum present at any meeting.

APPENDIX F

BYLAWS OF ADVISORY MANAGEMENT

LINE MATERIAL COMPANY
ELECTRICAL EQUIPMENT MANUFACTURERS MULTI-PLANT
OPERATION, HEADQUARTERS: MILWAUKEE, WISCONSIN

FOREWORD

The purpose of this Organization is to promote among its Members, a better understanding of all phases of Line Material Company business and its problems, and to place before Management for its approval positive programs and suggestions for improvements beneficial to the entire Line Material Organization.

SECTION I.

A. The name of the organization is Advisory Management.

SECTION II. Organization

A. The Officers' Committee is composed of all Vice Presidents and the Treasurer of Line Material Company (Delaware).

    1. The Chairman thereof is appointed by the Line Material Company Delaware President and serves for a term of six months starting January 1 to July 1, or until his successor is appointed.

    2. The Chairman appoints a secretary from the membership of the Officers' Committee. His term coincides with the term of the Chairman.

B. Initially Advisory Management is composed of:

    1. A Milwaukee and Barton Pool.

    2. A South Milwaukee Pool.

    3. A Milwaukee-Barton Board of 10 members including a Chairman and a Secretary.

    4. A South Milwaukee Board of 10 members including a Chairman and a Secretary.

5. The Executive Council consisting of the Chairmen and Secretaries of the Boards.

C. Other Line Material plants or subsidiaries may be brought under Advisory Management at the discretion of the Officers' Committee. They shall be established and operated on the same basis as provided herein for the Milwaukee Office and South Milwaukee and Barton Plants.

SECTION III. Membership

A. The Officers' Committee shall determine membership in accordance with the provisions set forth below:
1. Membership is limited to Salaried Employees.
2. Membership is further limited to employees holding jobs with job evaluation points of 100 or over.
3. The membership as it stands on October 20, 1947 shall remain standing for the fiscal year expiring June 30, 1948, subject to any discontinuance in case of employment termination, transfer into ineligible work, or resignation.
4. At the May, 1948 meeting of the Officers' Committee, there will be a review of the membership and a determination of membership for the fiscal year to commence July 1, 1948, and thereafter the same procedure shall be followed annually. Recommendations as to membership shall be submitted on a confidential basis by the Executive Council. The annual selection of Pool members shall then be guided by the following:
   a. Interest and participation in Advisory Management activities.
   b. Rating of the positions held with respect to the Federal Wage-Hour Act, it being the intent to limit Pool membership to employees engaged in executive, administrative or professional work exempt from overtime rights in the Federal law.

B. Board Members shall be selected by the Officers' Committee from their respective Pools.
1. Five members of the initial Board at any plant shall serve for a period of six months. The remaining five members

shall serve for a period of one year. Terms shall start January 1 and July 1.

2. All subsequent appointments shall be made for one-year terms except in the case of an appointment made to fill a vacancy occurring before the normal expiration period. Such interim appointment shall be for the unexpired term only.

3. No Board Member shall be eligible for re-appointment until six months have elapsed since the expiration date of his previous term except in the case of an interim appointee whose service as such did not exceed six months.

4. A Board Member is dropped automatically by three avoidable absences from Board Meetings in a six-months' period.

5. Replacements for retiring Board Members may be recommended to the Officers' Committee by their respective Boards. Recommendations must be presented at least 30 days in advance of retirement. Approval will be left to the discretion of the Officers' Committee.

SECTION IV. Meetings

A. The Executive Council with Officers' Committee approval shall call a general meeting of all eligible members, the Officers' Committee and other Company officers at least four times annually, March, June, September and December.

1. The Officers of each Board shall alternate as presiding Officers of general meetings.

2. As new Boards are created the Chairman of the Executive Council shall determine the order in which the new Board Officers shall serve as presiding officer of the general meetings.

B. The Executive Council shall hold at least one meeting each month on regular schedule as agreed upon by it members.

C. Each Board shall normally meet twice a month on regular schedule as agreed upon by the respective Boards.

D. Joint meetings of the Boards shall be called at the discretion of the Executive Council and may be substituted for regular local board meetings.

E. Minutes of all meetings shall be distributed in writing to all concerned at least one week prior to the next regular scheduled meeting.

    1. All corrections must be presented to the Secretary in writing prior to the next meeting. If there are no objections or corrections, the minutes will stand approved as written.

F. A majority of the membership of the above groups shall constitute a quorum.

SECTION V. Guests

A. It is the privilege of the Officers' Committee to invite guests to any general meeting.

B. The Executive Council, on application of any Eligible Pool Member, may invite guests to any meeting listed in Section IV.

C. Guests shall have no voting privileges.

SECTION VI. Procedure

A. Duties and responsibilities of the Executive Council shall be:

    1. To review and consider any recommendation of any Board or of the Joint Boards and thereupon to recommend, reject, or refer back for further study such recommendation. To present any recommendation finally approved by majority vote of the Executive Council to the Officers' Committee on the standard form provided for that purpose. Whenever the Executive Council rejects a recommendation of a Board, or of the Joint Boards, that rejection can be overridden by a unanimous vote of the Board or Joint Board membership (excluding the votes of Executive Council Members) and the matter thereupon submitted to the Officers' Committee on the basis of non-approval by the Executive Council.

    2. To review and consider any problem referred to the Executive Council by the Officers' Committee and report to the Officers' Committee the recommendation and thoughts of the Executive Council.

    3. To nominate Joint Project Task Committees. After such nominations are approved by the respective Boards, the

Executive Council shall appoint the required committee members.

4. To suggest specific local or joint studies to the Boards.

5. The Chairman of one Board and the Secretary of another Board shall alternate in attending Officers' Committee Meetings to explain and discuss the recommendation and other business as scheduled for such meetings.

6. The date of any Officers' Committee Meeting will be scheduled at least three weeks in advance by the Chairman thereof and the Executive Council shall, at least one week prior to such date, deliver to the Chairman or Secretary of the Officers' Committee the following:

   a. Seven copies of an agenda of the matters to be brought up for Officers' Committee consideration and action.

   b. Seven copies of the recommendations or reports to be considered, showing in any case, where the recommendation is made otherwise than by unanimous vote, a statement of the viewpoints of any who dissented.

B. Duties of Boards

1. Each Board shall elect from its Board Members a Chairman and Secretary to serve for a period of six months starting January 1 and July 1.

   a. The Chairman and Secretary may be re-elected.

   b. The Board Chairman shall nominate his respective Local Task Committee members and Committee Chairmen from his respective Pool.

2. Each Board shall normally meet twice a month on regular schedule as agreed upon by the respective Boards.

3. A written report of the action taken on any Pool member recommendation shall be presented to the Pool Member by the respective Board of Executive Council Secretary within 3 weeks after receipt of the recommendation.

4. Boards shall initiate Projects, define their scope and serve in an advisory capacity to Task Committees.

5. Boards shall have the power to approve or disapprove all Task Committee Members and Committee Chairmen

nominated from their respective Pools by either the Board Chairman or the Executive Council.

6. Boards shall receive from Task Committees all progress and final reports.

7. Boards shall receive and discuss final project reports.
   a. Preliminary discussion shall be held at one meeting and a tentative vote taken.
   b. Final discussion and final vote shall be taken no sooner than at the next Board meeting.
   c. Upon final approval, the Boards shall transmit the recommendation to the Executive Council.

8. No recommendation shall be given to the Executive Council until it has received at least a 75% favorable vote of the Board endorsing the recommendation. In any case where one or more members disagree with the recommendation, they may make a statement of their reasons for disagreement and transmit such statement to the Executive Council. Dissenters' statements as well as the approved statements of the majority may be unsigned.

C. Task Committees

1. Local Project Task Committee members and Committee Chairmen shall be nominated by the Board Chairman, approved by the Board and finally appointed by the Board Chairman.

2. Joint Project Task Committee members and Committee Chairmen shall be nominated by the Executive Council subject to the approval by each Board. Subsequent appointment shall be made by the Executive Council Chairman.

3. All Task Committee Members and Committee Chairmen must be Pool Members.

4. Each Task Committee shall select a Secretary.

5. The Task Committee responsible for presenting a specific project to the Boards shall make definite recommendations in writing to the Boards after discussion of the subject.
   a. Task Committees for local projects report to their respective Boards.

     b. Joint Task Committees present their reports at a Joint Board meeting.

     c. The Chairman of each Task Committee shall make a written progress report to his Board or Executive Council (if a Joint Project) at least once a month or upon special request from his Board or executive Council Chairman.

     d. A recommendation by a Task Committee may propose acceptable alternatives where more than one satisfactory solution to a problem is approved.

D. Recommendations by Pool Members to Boards

  1. Pool members may make recommendations to their respective Boards in the following manner:

     a. Written requests to any Board Member and if a Pool member so desires, he shall be accorded a reasonable hearing before the Board.

SECTION VII. Changes in By-Laws

A. Proposed changes in the By-Laws may be initiated by any Pool member in accordance with the general recommendation procedure as set forth in Section VI, Paragraph D.

  1. The proposed change shall be considered at the next joint board meeting.

B. The Joint Boards by a three-fourths vote of all members may promulgate a change in the By-Laws, which shall become effective immediately after approval by the Officers' Committee.

C. An amendment to these By-Laws may also be effected by the Officers' Committee, as follows:

  1. Any amendment adopted at any Officers' Committee meeting will be delivered in writing to the Executive Council within ten days after such Officers' Meeting and if no objection is received by the Chairman of the Officers Committee within thirty days after such delivery, the amendment will stand; but, if an objection is received, the amendment will be reconsidered at the next Officers' Committee meeting and the action then taken by way of affirmance, retraction or modification may at their option be final.

D. Amendments initiated by the Boards presented by the Executive Council may be approved, disapproved, or revised by the Officers' Committee.

Section VIII. General Rules

A. No questionnaire shall be used among Line Material employees nor shall any publicity by way of any letters, bulletin board notices, or newspaper releases be directed to Line Material employees or to the public, until same has been submitted to and approved by the Officers' Committee. This does not refer to ordinary notices of meetings.

B. Any Task Committee, upon undertaking the study of a project, shall initially advise the head of any department or plant concerned with the study. Task Committee members shall duly inform their immediate supervisors of the task or project they are undertaking.

APPENDIX G

SUPERVISORY PARTICIPATION PROGRAM

BIGELOW-SANFORD CARPET CO., INC.
NEW YORK, N. Y.

INTRODUCTION

In order to carry out the supervisory participation method used at the Berkshire Conference of 1947 and to provide a clearinghouse for the ideas of our supervisory forces and foremen for the expression of their opinions and suggestions on management problems, a program of representative boards will be set up.

COMPOSITION OF THE BOARDS

There shall be two separate and distinct boards at each plant and they will be known as the Council and the Assembly.

The Council shall consist of five men holding the rank of superintendent or its equivalent. The supervisory personnel of comparable rank of staff departments shall be eligible for membership on the Board provided they are responsible to the Plant Manager.

The Assembly shall consist of ten men made up of members of the supervisory personnel possessing the rank of overseers, foremen or their equivalent. Staff supervisors of overseer or foremen rank are also eligible.

The members of each board will be selected so that as many departments as possible are represented. The objective is to obtain maximum departmental coverage throughout the plant.

SELECTION OF THE ORIGINAL BOARD

The original members of the Council at each plant will be selected by the Plant Manager of that plant. The Council in turn will choose the original members of the Assembly with overseer and foreman representation equivalent to the total relationship of these two levels of supervision at each plant.

It is suggested that men who have demonstrated their interest in management problems as well as men conversant with the technical aspects of the business be given first consideration.

ROTATION OF BOARD MEMBERS

After the original boards have been selected the rotation of members will be accomplished by a system of self-rating and election. The membership retained and renewed on each board is as follows:

Council
3 men retained
2 men elected

Assembly
5 men retained
5 men elected

In order to select the members to be retained, each member will rate every other member excluding himself. This method of rating will be developed by the boards with the assistance of the Man Power Director. The retained members will then select the new members by methods to be determined, keeping in mind the departmental distribution and the rank relationship of the original boards.

THE FUNCTIONS OF THE BOARDS

The boards shall consider problems of the all-over operation of the plant. The boards are free to discuss any subject and make recommendations on any phase of management. In the event that a board should consider a technical subject within the normal province of a staff department, a member of that staff should be included on any investigatory committee.

The main business of the board is to develop an outlet for the thoughts, ideas and suggestions of the supervisory group. Either board has the authority to originate a problem for study or make a suggestion.

While the Council might of itself wish to instigate certain projects it will be their normal function to turn these over to the Assembly for study and recommendation. All recommendations from the Assembly to the Council shall be unanimous. The same recommendation shall be passed on unanimously by the Council before it is presented to the Plant Manager for action. The Plant Manager may return the recommendation to the Council with his recommendations for reconsideration. In the event that the Plant Manager ultimately rejects a recommendation a statement of his reason for such rejection shall be presented in writing to the Council Chairman and the Vice President in Charge of Manufacturing.

ORGANIZATION OF THE BOARDS

A chairman shall be elected by the Board from its own members at the first regular meeting of each new Board. A secretary will be provided by the Management and will not be a member of the Board nor have any vote or voice in the proceedings. Elections for the chairman shall be made by separate written ballot by the Board members. The Chairman shall be chief executive officer of the Board. He shall preside at all meetings, shall have general supervision and delegation of all its activities and committees and shall be an ex-officio member of all standing and appointed committees; shall have all power and authorities usually vested in the authority of chairmanship. In addition he shall appoint members of sub-committees and shall see that all members of the Board receive their fee at the termination of each meeting.

The secretary shall keep the records of the Board, give proper notices to all members of the group and perform all other duties as may be described by the Chairman. He shall record votes and the minutes of the proceedings in a book kept for the purpose. In addition the Secretary shall keep a record of the status of each project which is before the Board and properly prepare the report on each completed project for transmission to the next step.

In the absence of the Chairman those present on the Board will elect a chairman pro tem for the period of his absenteeism.

MEETINGS

There shall be at least two regularly scheduled meetings each month in the quarters designated by the Management. These meetings shall be held at 3 p.m. on a day of the week best suited to the convenience of the Board and shall extend for a period of not more than two hours. Additional meetings may be called by the Chairman or a majority of the Board at any time when considered necessary

An attendance of the majority of regular members will constitute a quorum at any meeting.

TENURE OF OFFICE

The life of any Board shall be for a period of nine months.

FEES OF THE BOARD MEMBERS

All members of the Council shall receive a fee of $10 for attendance at a regularly scheduled meeting.

Members of the Assembly shall receive a fee of $5 for attendance at a regularly scheduled meeting.

These fees shall be free and clear of all deductions such as withholding taxes, social security, etc.

ANNUAL MEETING OF ALL BOARD MEMBERS

Once a year a combined meeting of all members who have served on each board at each plant will take place at a selected point. The President of the company, the Vice President in Charge of Manufacturing, the Plant Managers and any other invited members of the Operations Committee should be present at this meeting.

This meeting will be presided over by the current Chairman of the Council of the plant where the immediate meeting takes place.

At this meeting the results of all Board activities for the year will be reported on by each Board from each plant.

June 1, 1948.

INDEX

133